THE
INFORMATION CONTINUUM

D1566912

THE
INFORMATION
CONTINUUM

Evolution of Social Information Transfer
in Monkeys, Apes, and Hominids

BARBARA J. KING

A School of American Research Resident Scholar Book
SAR PRESS · SANTA FE · NEW MEXICO

SCHOOL OF AMERICAN RESEARCH PRESS
Post Office Box 2188
Santa Fe, New Mexico 87504-2188

Distributed by the University of Washington Press

Library of Congress Cataloging-in-Publication Data:
King, Barbara J., 1956–
    The information continuum : evolution of social information transfer in
monkeys, apes, and hominids / Barbara J. King. -- 1st ed.
        p. cm.
    "A School of American Research resident scholar book."
    Includes bibliographical references (p.) and index.
    ISBN 0-933452-39-X (cloth). -- ISBN 0-933452-40-3 (paper)
    1. Human evolution. 2. Communication. 3. Animal communication.
4. Man, Prehistoric. 5. Primates--Behavior. I. Title.
GN281.4.K48 1994
    302.2--dc20   94-1690
                                                  CIP

Cover: Rhesus macaque females surround a five-day-old infant. The three adults
are, from left, the infant's grandmother, mother, and aunt. Photo taken at Cayo
Santiago, Puerto Rico, by Courtney A. Snyder. Courtesy Courtney A. Snyder.

FOR
CHARLIE

CONTENTS

ILLUSTRATIONS AND TABLES

Illustrations

Tables

ACKNOWLEDGMENTS

All my life, I've loved books, not only for their contents but also for their look, feel, and newly-minted—or old-musty—smell. Creating my first book has been a special experience, and I'd like to mark its completion by thanking the people who have helped make it happen.

Chapter three is based on my dissertation, and hence on my fieldwork at Amboseli, Kenya, in 1985–86. I am grateful to those individuals who gave me the chance to study wild baboons and who provided intellectual or logistical guidance during those 14 months—Stuart Altmann, Jeanne Altmann, Amy Samuels, Phillip Muruthi, and Raphael Mututua. The Kenyan people and government, including the Kajiado County Council, graciously supported my research. Major financial support for fieldwork came from my dissertation-improvement NSF grant (#BNS-8512247) and an NIMH grant (15007) to Jeanne Altmann. I also received funding from the University of Oklahoma Research Associates' Fund and the Foundation for Research into the Origin of Man. Special thanks for friendship during a difficult time in the field go to Lynne Isbell.

My doctoral committee at the University of Oklahoma—Jane Lancaster (now of the University of New Mexico), Stephen Thompson, Troy Abell, Bedford Vestal, and Paul Minnis—improved my dissertation via many helpful suggestions. I am grateful to Trish Schagmeyer and Doug Mock, also of the University of Oklahoma, who helped me understand a great deal about theory, methods, and data analysis in the study of animal behavior, and who fed me in Norman often and well. For statistical and computer-related help, I thank Cynthia Null and Burt Avery at the College of William and Mary.

Most of my dissertation writing was completed while I was a Resident Scholar at the School of American Research in Santa Fe. A Weatherhead Predoctoral Fellowship allowed me to write in a place of quiet beauty, surrounded by mountains and the best next-door neighbors anywhere. From that year (1987–88) at SAR I thank Doug Schwartz, Jonathan Haas, Jane Kepp, Cecile Stein, and fellow Resident Scholars Richard G. Fox and Glenn Stone. Later,

Jane Kepp—first of SAR Press and now of Kepp Editorial—masterfully edited the entire manuscript of this book. It would be impossible to exaggerate her efficiency and ability to grasp and articulate what I'd wanted to say all along. For advice and encouragment in the latter stages of book production, I am grateful to Joan O'Donnell and the rest of the staff at SAR Press.

The ideas presented in this book stem mainly from my recent thinking and writing about the evolution of cognition and communication. I've been influenced a great deal by the work of B. G. Galef and Kathleen Gibson. For discussion of ideas and/or access to unpublished data or ideas, I thank Carol Berman, Kathleen Gibson, Bill McGrew, Willow Powers, and Janette Wallis. Wayne McGuire provided a critical reference on teaching in animals at a critical time. Bill McGrew and an anonymous reviewer for SAR Press improved the manuscript immeasurably with constructive, perceptive suggestions. Karen and Ronald Flowe read and improved early drafts of two chapters; for making me believe I should keep on with writing, and for inaugurating our wonderful Writing Group, I thank them.

Anthropology students at The College of William and Mary provided library and research assistance. I particularly appreciate the efficient work of Valerie Dean, Kerry Saltmarsh Harkins, Michael Sharpless, and Courtney Snyder. Rebecca Brooks took on the mess otherwise known as my bibliographic material, and with only a popcorn box and her own considerable skill, succeeded in organizing it and me. For that feat, for reading and editing the manuscript, and for three years of good talks about primatology, I thank her.

For permission to use their superb photographs, I thank Janette Wallis and Courtney Snyder.

Special appreciation is reserved for two people. Jane Lancaster continues to be my primary mentor, as she has since 1979. I have benefited immensely from her insight into a wide variety of issues, and from her generous sharing of time and resources. At William and Mary, I have Talbot Taylor to thank for sharing unconventional ideas about language, and for humor in the Willliamsburg trenches; for persistently, graciously disagreeing with me on many things (but for agreeing on many more); and for dragging me into the E-mail era.

For supporting me—in all senses of the word—I thank my parents, Elizabeth King and the late Walter King. For all our talks, and for guiding me in more ways than they know, I thank Cahlene Cramer, Virginia Kerns, Heather MacDonald, Vicki Kirsch, and Mary Voigt. My deepest thanks are reserved for my husband, Charles Hogg. For his endless willingness to discuss my ideas, half-baked and otherwise, for sharing with me Sarah, three incomparable cats, books, and travel, and for making our life together the best kind of adventure, I dedicate this book to him.

THE
INFORMATION CONTINUUM

I

SOCIAL INFORMATION TRANSFER

Humans today, especially in industrialized countries, are bombarded with information conveyed by technology over vast distances. Telephones are available in cars and airplanes; televisions transmit to our living rooms events and images of war as they occur. In remote areas of Africa, the names of British and American rock stars are widely known. An entire profession—data processing—devotes itself exclusively to the managing of information via technology.

We may try to escape such information overload. "Getting away from it all" usually means escaping the burdens of too-efficient information flow. Avoiding information is ironic for a species molded by a long evolutionary history to be able to give and receive ever larger quantities of information in ever more complex ways. For anthropologists, the fascinating aspect of information transfer is not our newfound struggle to cope with information overload but our long-term struggle as primates to obtain, use, and transfer information efficiently.

For millions of years, primates have been shaped by natural selection for efficient gathering and use of information. For primates, as for most animals, information is a critical resource for survival and reproduction. Critical resources are usually thought of as tangible items such as food, water, shelter, mates, and allies. But seeking and using these resources present problems that animals must solve in their daily lives—and what permits the resources to be sought, found, and used appropriately is information.

Individuals may acquire information from the environment entirely through their own senses and apply it directly to problem solving. They may have to risk trial-and-error experimentation to find the most efficient application of the information to the problem. For group-living animals, however, a vastly more efficient method is to get information from more experienced members of the same species (hereafter called *conspecifics*). Doing so is not without costs, including the risk of deception, but in general, more information can be gained more quickly this way, and chances for making dangerous errors associated with trial-and-error behavior are reduced.

Such *social* information transfer—along with, more generally, the evolution of communication—is the subject of this book. Social information transfer is a form of communication, and the broad framework used here is based on the evolution of communication in primates. I will focus on the monkeys and apes (hereafter *primates*) and on our prehistoric human ancestors living between about 4 million and 10,000 years ago (hereafter *hominids*) and will compare them to each other and to modern humans in various aspects of social information transfer and communication.

Information Donation and Acquisition

The main argument I wish to make is that in the long evolutionary history of our species there has been a gradual, incremental development of the ability to donate information to others, culminating in the human ability to transfer massive amounts of information through our species-specific forms of teaching. Information donation may be accomplished in many ways, including deliberate sending of specific messages, explicit encouragement or discouragement of certain actions, and intervention in or demonstration of various behaviors. Hypothetical examples of information donation include those of an adult monkey warning its offspring of approaching danger by directing a specific alarm call toward them; an adult ape reaching out to remove an item of food from her younger sister's hand, preventing the sibling from eating it; and an educator lecturing to a roomful of college students.

In each of these examples, one individual, whom we can label *A,* in some way is more experienced or possesses more knowledge than another (or others), labeled *B. A* may, of course, be more experienced in one dimension and *B* more experienced in another, so that in different situations the same animal may play reverse roles. An important criterion for information donation is that *A* acts in some direct way specifically toward *B*. We can even say that *A* acts in a way consistent with an *intent* to communicate and donate information to *B*. Measuring intent, however, is a tricky issue, and the presence of intent is not a requirement for information donation, as I discuss more fully later. What is important is that as a result of *A*'s acting toward *B, B* receives, either actually or potentially, more information than it would otherwise.

Information may, of course, pass from *A* to *B* without action directed by *A* toward *B*. When information is transferred this way—in the absence of information donation—the type of transfer involved may be called social information acquisition. Although in social information acquisition, a less experienced animal still interacts with a more experienced one and emerges with more information, there is one critical difference from information donation: *A* allows *B* to observe or interact with it, but does not act directly toward *B* and seemingly has no intent to communicate with *B*. Furthermore, *A* is more likely to incur a cost (for example, in energy expenditure) in the case of information donation than in information acquisition (see also Caro and Hauser 1992).

Consider the case of an ape feeding at a fruiting fig tree. The ape *A* approaches the tree quietly and, as it begins to feed, is quickly surrounded by other apes, including an infant, *B*. The infant observes what *A* eats and how *A* prepares figs before ingesting them; it may also pick up and eat small scraps of fig that fall onto *A*'s fur and around *A*'s body. *A* is aware of *B*'s behavior but does not react toward *B* at all, neither threatening nor encouraging *B*. In this case, *B* is likely to get information from *A* about diet and feeding behavior, but *A* has not donated information to *B*.

Sometimes *A* and *B* are both adults—for example, when a primate moves into a new group after puberty, as males do in many monkey populations. The new arrival confronts unfamiliar animals, some of which will be future allies, others, future rivals, and still others, future mates. The habitat and food sources of the new home range may differ from those of the male's natal group. In coping with these unfamiliar variables, the immigrant might well benefit from getting information known to its groupmates.

In most cases of social information transfer, though, the more experienced animal is an adult and the less experienced one an immature, that is, an infant or juvenile. For convenience in discussing social information transfer, I will therefore use the terms *adult* and *immature,* but the reader should keep in mind that the words "more experienced animal" and "less experienced animal" are more strictly accurate.

The major difference, then, in the two types of social information transfer (abbreviated here as *information donation* and *information acquisition*) rests in the relative roles of adults and immatures. In information acquisition, as defined here, infants take the primary responsibility for turning a social interaction (including mere toleration of proximity) into an opportunity for getting information. Their behaviors include some in which the immature takes a very active role—such as initiating interactions that result in acquisition of information—and others in which the immature merely attends to adult behavior, as in the earlier example of the ape in a fruiting tree. One of the key arguments in this book is that immature primates are active agents of their own socialization. Immatures may or may not play active roles in any particular instance of information acquisition, but in many cases they have the ability to affect the course of their own development (Baldwin 1986; Dolhinow 1991) and are capable of much more than the passive observation with which they are usually credited.

Another key assertion is that information is donated by adults to immatures in more diverse contexts and more sophisticated ways as one moves from consideration of primates to hominids to humans. These shifts are quantitative, however, not qualitative. I view the evolution of communication in primates and hominids as a gradual process in which certain abilities were increasingly selected for: the ability to recognize the benefits of donation of information to immatures, to find diverse ways to accomplish that donation, and to store or accumulate the knowledge that resulted from successive acts of donation. This gradualist perspective sets me apart from quite a few anthropologists, other scientists, and writers who suggest that the "watershed" separating humans and other primates is the relatively recent development of human speech and language. I will develop this gradualist approach in various ways throughout the book.

In chapters 2 and 3, I discuss recent data from primate behavior research, including my own study of infant baboons in Kenya, in order to show that information acquisition by immatures—not information donation by adults—is the major method of social information transfer in primates. Adults do sometimes donate information to immatures, including their own offspring; these exceptional instances are described in order to understand more fully the pattern and its exceptions. Arguably, the most remarkable report of information donation involves the active teaching of tool-use techniques by some chimpanzee mothers in a population in Ivory Coast (Boesch 1991).

From the perspective of evolutionary theory, it is puzzling that such instances are so infrequent. Primate parents, especially mothers, invest a tremendous amount of energy in rearing their young. Single births are the rule. Offspring are nurtured and protected by the mother and sometimes by other family members during the period of infant dependency, which, depending on the species, may last from a few months to over four years. That this nurturing rarely includes information donation seems counterintuitive. If a mother could help her offspring by donating information to it at relatively little cost to herself, why doesn't she? Primatologists have no true understanding of this situation.

In chapter 4, I look at social information transfer in our human ancestors. I ask how hominid capabilities for this behavior, particularly information donation, differ from those of primates, and how such abilities might be measured. Hominids did not, of course, evolve from apes, but they shared a common ancestor with some great apes as recently as 5 million years ago. In order to make full use of the evolutionary perspective, hominid behavior and hominid material culture, such as tools and art, must be examined for evidence of the relative roles of immatures and adults in information transfer. Doing so strengthens the conclusion that in understanding the evolution of communication, a critical factor is the evolving ability of adults to donate information to immatures. It also strengthens the view that no critical watershed in social information transfer separates primates and humans.

I feel optimistic that as archaeological techniques become more sophisticated, we will be able to learn a great deal more about hominid communication. Moreover, data will continue to accumulate from studies of primates around the world. From these two sources we may learn about additional instances of information donation in nonhumans, including some that are totally unexpected. Such new data would not weaken the point of view adopted here. My argument emphatically does not rest on the assumption that some form of social information transfer is unique to humans.

The first four chapters of the book, then, are descriptive. Chapter 5 continues with a brief consideration of social information transfer in modern humans, but then shifts to explanation by discussing some possible reasons for the evolution of increased information donation. My focus is on reasons for differences between information donation in monkeys and some great apes, on the one hand, and some great apes and early hominids, on the other. One likely selection pressure for increased information donation was greater dependence on what Parker and Gibson (1979) have called tool-aided extractive foraging, or using tools to obtain "hidden" or embedded food items such as those that grow underground or are encased in hard shells. Other factors to be considered are cognitive rather than ecological. Although I focus heavily on the relationship between foraging strategies and the evolution of increased information donation, I close chapter 5 with mention of some alternative hypotheses.

In the sixth and final chapter, I confront the question of human uniqueness. My conclusions about the evolution of information donation are relevant for current debates about human uniqueness, continuity or discontinuity in the evolution of language, and other issues that touch on primate intelligence. Predictions about human uniqueness are often made confidently by anthropologists, psychologists, linguists, and writers of popular science books, only to be falsified after a few years of scrutiny by primatologists and other ethologists (Gibson 1990). In the last 40 years alone it has been claimed that of all primates (and in some cases, of all species on earth), only humans use or make tools, hunt meat in a cooperative fashion, communicate referentially or by using symbols, or exhibit self-awareness. Each of these behaviors has since been discovered in one or several primate species, and there is no reason to think that the situation will be any different for information donation. Indeed, as I commented earlier, my view is that any differences in social information transfer among primates, hominids, and modern humans are ones of degree, not kind (King 1991). Although this position is still not widespread among anthropologists, it has been around at least since Darwin and now enjoys something of a renaissance within anthropology, as I will show.

Key Concepts

Definitions of key concepts must be provided next, but as anyone who has grappled with defining complex behaviors will appreciate, this is a difficult task. The literature abounds with widely disparate views of what is meant by information, social information transfer, communication, referential or symbolic communication, and social learning. As every student of introductory anthropology learns, more than 160 definitions of culture had already been compiled 40 years ago (Kroeber and Kluckhohn 1952), and they have multiplied since then. The problem is not limited to concepts like culture that are usually applied to humans alone (but see Bonner 1980). Galef (1988:11), for instance, catalogs no fewer than 22 terms, each with its own nuance of meaning, that refer to various types of learning by imitation. In the face of such terminological proliferation, it is doubly important to operationalize terms. If committing myself to certain definitions instead of others results in spirited discussion among readers, that is all to the good, for that is how definitions and arguments are improved.

In addition to defining terms, I will discuss the relationships among social information transfer, communication, learning, and teaching. The final section of this first chapter is devoted to a brief summary of the basic anatomical and social adaptations of primates and to a consideration of how the evolutionary perspective adopted here relates to use of primate models in anthropology.

Information and Communication

Smith's (1977:2) definition of information as "that which permits choices to be made" is a good starting point for explaining what I mean by this term. Any sensory input that allows an animal to decide among behavioral options is information, according to Smith's definition. Some people, especially those who study humans, may associate the use of information, and hence behavioral choice making, with the so-called "higher animals." They may expect choice making to be restricted to vertebrates, or perhaps to birds and mammals only. Bonner (1980) convincingly challenges such chauvinism by looking, surprisingly enough, at bacteria. He describes how bacteria choose among alternative behaviors and concludes that motile bacteria have been "seriously underestimated" in terms of their behavioral capability: "They can take quite complex readings of their immediate environment and directly translate the information into the appropriate directed movement" (1980:64).

How does this use of information include choosing among alternatives? Consider one experiment conducted by Berg and Koshland (cited in Bonner 1980). Normally, bacteria locomote by random motion composed of straight-line movements interspersed with "tumbling" movements. A bacterial cell may be confronted simultaneously with a repellant and an attractant:

> The cells have specific receptor proteins for both, and apparently they will respond to both simultaneously if the concentrations are properly adjusted. The double gradient will be equivalent to no gradient at all as far as the cell is concerned, and it will move randomly. The two separate bits of external information are somehow integrated and a compromise is reached. (Bonner 1980:64)

Thus, the bacterium "chose" to behave a certain way; it conceivably could have reacted differently. For example, it could have first responded in a way appropriate to a repellant and then in a way appropriate to an attractant, with rapid alternation between the two.

That bacteria move in a certain way based on information is fascinating, but these data nonetheless beg the real question of choice, since no one claims that bacteria are capable of brain-mediated decisions. Nonetheless, the data from bacteria lead to an important point. Information is used by an enormous variety of species, and in order to discuss information transfer meaningfully, some distinctions must be drawn.

A monkey may look at, smell, touch, and/or taste a piece of fruit to assess its ripeness and suitability for eating, and thus get information about the environment directly through the senses. She can then decide whether or not to eat the fruit. As in the case of the bacterium, no other individuals are involved in the process. Presumably, had another bacterial cell been added to the gradient experiment, the process of obtaining and using information would not have been altered; the first cell could not have communicated information to the second about what response to make. A monkey, however, can get information about the availability and condition of food from her social companions and would very likely benefit, in terms of speed of transmission and error reduction, as a result.

Although definitions of the two types of social information transfer have been offered, I still have not tackled the more basic question, What is social information transfer itself? To start with a rigorous definition, I adopt Galef's (1988:13) description of what he calls social transmission: any social interaction that increases the probability that one individual will come independently to exhibit a behavior initially in the repertoire of another. Two or more animals are thus needed for social information transfer to take place. The recipient gets information from the environment and processes it through

9

the senses, as in any kind of information transfer, but now the information is channeled through another animal (the recipient's social environment).

Whenever one animal transfers information to another, not only social information transfer but also social communication occurs. By definition, then, the behavior of one individual has affected the behavior of others (S. Altmann 1967:326). The term *others* usually refers only to conspecifics and excludes interactions between animals of different species, such as predators and prey. Although predators may affect the behavior of their prey, these two classes of individuals are not part of the same society and so are not considered participants in social communication (S. Altmann 1967).

Treating social information transfer in this framework brings us back to the question of intent. Earlier I noted that in information donation, according to my definition, one animal acts in a way consistent with having an intent to donate information to another. This is because information donation is defined as "action directed toward an immature," including guidance, encouragement, discouragement, message sending through vocalizations, and so forth, and the usual assumption is that directed action is intentional action. But might directed action be possible without the intent to donate information? Two examples may help clarify this issue.

Imagine, first, a mother monkey slapping or biting her infant as the infant reaches for the food item the mother is about to eat. Clearly the slap or bite constitutes "directed action" (and thus intentional action) toward the infant. Furthermore, through the mother's directed action some information is most likely transferred to the infant about what it is and is not allowed to do with its mother's food. This example clearly constitutes information donation—but is the behavior necessarily intentional on the part of the mother? In some cases, it might be, and in others, not. Perhaps the mother is guiding the infant's food choice, but alternatively, the mother's only motivation may be to protect her own food supply.

Picture, second, an ape mother traveling with two immatures through the African forest and vocalizing upon sighting an abundant source of ripe fruit. Here the situation is more complicated, because it is not so obvious whether vocalizations are directed at particular individuals or not. One possibility is that the vocalization is not directed at anyone, but simply expresses the mother's emotional or arousal state. Another possibility is that the vocalization contains specific information about the fruit—for example, its ripeness—but the ape is directing the vocalization at all members of her social group and not at her offspring in particular. In each case, information transfer would occur via information acquisition and not information donation. (This example highlights the important point that action must be directed at immatures specifically, and not just conspecifics generally, to count as information donation.)

There are other possibilities, however. The ape may be directing her vocalization specifically at the immatures in order to inform them about the fruit; or she may be directing her vocalization at the immatures but without the intent to donate information (the motivation in this case is harder to guess; the example probably works only hypothetically). In both of these last possibilities, because information is transferred by directed action of the mother, we can make a case for information donation, but only the first would count as intentional information donation.

Underlying this example concerning vocalization is the issue of whether primates are capable only of emotional communication or also of referential communication (Steklis 1985; Seyfarth 1986; Snowdon 1990). *Emotional communication* is a shorthand term that assumes an animal conveys only its state of arousal. The animal does so involuntarily and, as a result, honestly, without withholding or altering information. In referential communication, which is usually conceived of as occurring in the vocal-auditory mode, some specific information about the environment is conveyed to others. The animal goes beyond mere reporting of what it feels; the communication is voluntary and may not always be honest. Examples of referential communication would include vocalizations that report the presence of ripe fruit or of a certain kind of dangerous predator. In such cases, more than hunger or fear is being reported, and information may be falsified.

Entrenched in anthropology for decades was a perspective that strictly dichotomized emotional and referential communication. It rejected out of hand the claim that any primate could communicate referentially:

> While human language was assumed to be under voluntary, higher
> cortical control, and human words assumed to represent objects or
> events in the external world, observers described the vocalizations
> of monkeys and apes as occurring only in highly emotional circum-
> stances, such as fights or encounters with predators. It was concluded
> that nonhuman primate vocalizations were relatively involuntary,
> under limited higher cortical control, and that such calls could not
> be interpreted as "representing" anything other than an individual's
> internal emotional state. (Seyfarth 1986:440)

Although primatologists still have no clear idea of the relative roles played by emotional and referential communication among primates, it can no longer be doubted that some primates can communicate referentially, voluntarily, and deceptively (as, indeed, Steklis showed conclusively in 1985). Evidence for these claims will be laid out thoroughly in later chapters. For the moment, the important point is how these abilities relate to the question of intent and information donation.

The question of intent in information transfer is interesting but not directly relevant to my key arguments. I make no assumptions about the presence or absence of intent in any given case of information transfer. In many cases (such as directed vocalizations), directed action and information donation may be synonymous; in others (such as directed discouragement), they may not be. Although I will not be concerned with making this distinction, it is a worthwhile area for further study. Knowing for certain whether a case of information donation includes intent would seem to depend, in most cases, on experimental verification rather than just observation or listening—and here we are back to the question of how to measure intent. One promising method is to demonstrate that adults increase information donation when in the presence of immatures who could benefit from that information (see Cheney and Seyfarth 1990:chapters 2 and 3). Finding a way to measure *absence* of intent is yet another challenge for primatologists.

To encourage hypothesis testing and experimentation, a hierarchy of levels for assessing intentionality in primate communication can be created. Boehm (1989) suggests that an animal might (1) advertise emotional states only; (2) communicate information about its social and physical environment; (3) intend to communicate so that the information transmitted has an effect upon the hearer; and (4) communicate intentionally in matters that involve displacement in time and space. Such hierarchies (see also Dennett 1987), however constructed as to detail, should encourage precise and valuable work in the future.

Other questions remain to be answered (or, at least, asked) about social information transfer. Even if communication is intentional, how can we know that the behavior of others has been affected by the process of information transfer? How can this effect be measured? Are there cases in which one individual intends to communicate in order to affect another's behavior but fails to achieve the intended effect? To attempt to answer these questions, social information transfer must be compared to social learning.

Social Information Transfer and Learning

For primatologists who imagine or observe immature primates going about their lives and trying to solve everyday problems, the process of social learning probably comes to mind before social information transfer. After all, the classic type of statement on infant development highlights the role of learning, almost always described as passive observation of social companions (but see Boyd and Richerson 1985; Baldwin 1986; Dolhinow 1991). Social learning obviously can be important in primate infant development. (The term *social learning* is not monolithic; it subsumes several behaviors, each different from the next. Since my arguments do not depend on classifying these different types, I refer the interested reader to reviews of social learning [e.g., Hall 1963; Beck 1980; Galef 1988].)

But how is social learning different from social information transfer? Does a focus on social information transfer eliminate the need to discuss social learning? The key distinction between the two has been made by Galef (1988). Strict criteria must be fulfilled in order to claim that social learning is responsible for the appearance of a new behavior in an animal (see also Beck 1980; Galef 1991). The most stringent requirement is that the new behavior must be adopted as a direct result of social interaction with conspecifics. Ideally, then, the scientist interested in social learning must observe the very first occurrence of the behavior in the naive animal. This requirement presents a significant challenge for the animal behaviorist (but see Russon and Galdikas 1993, and the discussion of imitation as social learning in chapter 3). When is it possible to be certain that the first time one sees a certain behavior, it is also the first time the animal has performed the behavior? Confidence about meeting this criterion is probably highest when one works with a captive population for which animals' histories are known, and when behavior is either controlled experimentally (animals have limited access to objects and companions that could affect the behavior in question) or monitored around the clock.

Experimental manipulation that allows testing of critical variables in the field is rarely carried out on primates. Very few (if any) research projects concentrate intensively on one or two individuals long enough to monitor social learning. Such an intensive approach, advocated by Strum (1988), has been adopted for brief periods in studies unrelated to learning. For example, two of Goodall's students at Gombe Stream Research Centre, Tanzania, demonstrated the feasibility and worth of concentrating on one chimpanzee at a time (Goodall 1990). Between them, David Riss and Curt Busse observed the chimpanzee Figan continuously for fifty days. As an adult, Figan had an incompletely known history; social learning could not have been studied reliably in this case.

Even if a subject's history is known, intensive observation still fails to eliminate all obstacles to the completeness required for the assessment of social learning. At night, for example, most primates make sleeping nests in trees or sleep on cliffs. Nighttime, however, is not an inactive period. Infants suckle from their mothers and may play with each other or with juveniles. At many sleeping sites, food is available; any study of diet and feeding behavior is technically incomplete unless data are taken during the night. Obtaining nighttime data is an unreasonable expectation for most field studies of primates, although it is obligatory for research on nocturnal species and may be accomplished with sophisticated equipment such as night scopes. Yet for studies of social learning, the issue cannot easily be dismissed for any species because incomplete observations prevent the primatologist from knowing when an animal first performed a behavior.

Difficulties like this one were brought home to me when, in 1985, I began to study the foraging behavior of infant baboons at Amboseli National Park, Kenya. This population of monkeys had been studied almost continuously since 1971 by Jeanne and Stuart Altmann of the University of Chicago and their colleagues (e.g., Altmann and Altmann 1970; Hausfater 1975; J. Altmann 1980). I was fortunate to be able to join a research project where animals were named and known as individuals. Many kinship relations had been worked out over the years, and plant foods in the area had been identified.

My plan was to build on this previous work by finding out when and how young infants supplement their diet of mother's milk with solid foods. How exactly do infants behave when they first encounter what are, for them, new foods in the environment? Do they eat only when and what the mother or some other experienced adult eats? Do they observe adults' food choices and processing techniques before selecting and preparing food items? Do they copy adults' motor patterns? Do they participate actively in getting information about diet—that is, in some way other than observation and imitation? In other words, I wanted to know whether infants learned their first food-related behaviors as a direct result of social interaction.

Aware that the ideal situation would be to see the first occurrence of a new behavior, I planned to observe one of the first few encounters between an infant and a particular food item. Because I wasn't trying to do anything as fancy as distinguish among types of social learning, this goal seemed feasible. The availability of baboon foods at Amboseli changes often, according to climatic variables such as rainfall (S. Altmann, personal communication), so there would be many times when new foods appeared for infants to encounter. Suppose, for example, that an infant baboon is born in August (three were, in fact, born during August 1986). Three months later, the infant still gets the bulk of its nutrition from mother's milk but spends some time away from the mother. During this time away, the infant sometimes samples and possibly ingests some solid foods. Perhaps at the start of the wet season (which in 1986 began in October), it samples some small berries that are favored by adults. Clearly, the infant could not have encountered these berries before because this is the first time they have been available since its birth. By intensively observing the infant, I should have been assured of seeing one of its first encounters with the berries.

Although I recorded observations relevant to my research questions, I never felt certain that I was seeing one of the first few encounters of infants with new foods. I did not take data at night—indeed, I had never planned to, and it was extremely difficult to discern what infants were doing in the dark high up in trees—and other problems cropped up as well. When observing an infant, I sometimes lost sight of it when it crawled under a thick bush or ran high up into a tree lush with blossoms. If the infant's mother sensed real or potential danger, she would scoop up the infant and gallop away in a cloud of dust. By the time I caught up with the pair, several minutes had often elapsed. All these problems resulted in gaps in the data.

More seriously, I could not watch intensively only one or two infants. Infant mortality at Amboseli is high—nearly 30 percent per year for the first two years of life (J. Altmann 1980:33). Had I chosen to observe only one or two infants, I would have risked losing my subjects partway through the study. Instead, I compared infants in two groups of baboons that ranged in different areas of the park, and so missed whole days with the infants of one group while I was with the other. (I did not observe baboons seven days a week, either.) These and related problems plague nearly every study of primates, or any other animal in the wild. They are not remarkable and perhaps not even noteworthy unless the focus of the study is one with strict requirements about when certain behaviors are observed, as is the case for social learning. In short, I found out for myself what the experts had said all along: it is nearly impossible to know the circumstances surrounding the appearance of a new behavior in an animal in the wild.

A focus on social information transfer gets around some of these obstacles. To claim that social information transfer is at work, social interaction between two or more animals must take place, but there are no constraints on when it happens (Galef 1988). That is, social interaction need not occur immediately before the appearance of a new behavior and need not be directly responsible for its adoption. Cases considered as social information transfer (or social transmission by Galef) involve those for which social interaction occurs but may not itself be a prerequisite for the new behavior to appear. An infant primate, for instance, might well learn how to avoid poisonous berries or other toxic foods even without social interaction, or through social interaction and nonsocial methods simultaneously. Perhaps the infant samples small bits of the food and learns partly through trial and error whether it is safe or not.

But when social interaction occurs and affects infant behavior in precise ways, social information transfer is involved. Strictly speaking, two important outcomes must be shown to exist before labeling anything as social information transfer. In Galef's terms, these are increased homogeneity of behavior of the interactants, and persistence of that homogeneity over time. These requirements mean that the behavior of the two individuals involved in the social interaction must increase in similarity, with the similarity extending beyond the social interaction itself.

Returning to the example of the baboon infant and the berries, the practical consequences for the scientist of shifting from social learning to social information transfer can be seen. All that must be demonstrated now are three things: that the infant interacts at some point with conspecifics; that after doing so, its diet in general (or its choice and use of berries in particular) conforms to the behaviors of those with whom it interacted; and that the conformity is maintained over time. Measuring these three things should be easier than demonstrating social learning in any reliable way. I say "should be" not because of any lack of confidence that it can be done, but because at present a big gap exists between theory and data: so far, few primatologists have collected evidence for the conditions listed by Galef as needed to invoke social information transfer.

Thus, a word of warning is in order: results reported in later chapters about social information transfer will not match up precisely with the criteria described here. In using the terms *information donation* and *information acquisition,* I make no claim that the ideal criteria have been fulfilled. Studies of social information transfer are not much farther along at the moment than studies of social learning, but we are dealing with a new concept (as defined strictly). As more primatologists (e.g., Hauser 1988) read Galef's work, they will collect the evidence needed to use the strict definition of social information transfer.

Teaching as Information Donation

So far, I have been using the term *teaching* casually as a word with an obvious meaning that fits the criteria for information donation. In fact, although teaching is typically defined in human terms and considered unique to humans (see the review in Caro and Hauser 1992), it can also be found in other animals. As is clear from recent emphases on theoretical considerations and empirical data on nonhuman teaching (e.g., Boesch 1991; Caro and Hauser 1992), the criterion of directed action in information donation is easily satisfied when one assesses teaching behavior using a good, precise definition—and without assuming that teaching is uniquely human. A revitalized study of teaching thus presents a promising avenue of research for studies of social information transfer.

Caro and Hauser's (1992:153) definition of teaching is the one I will adopt:

> An individual actor A can be said to teach if it modifies its behavior only in the presence of a naive observer, $B,$ at some cost or at least without obtaining an immediate benefit for itself. A's behavior thereby encourages or punishes B's behavior, or provides B with ex-

perience, or sets an example for *B*. As a result, *B* acquires knowledge or learns a skill earlier in life or more rapidly or efficiently than it might otherwise do, or that it would not learn at all.

In discussing key aspects of this definition, Caro and Hauser make some points that facilitate the comparison of teaching with information donation in general. First, in teaching, the teacher (an adult, in my terms) must modify its behavior only when a pupil (an immature) is present. This requirement immediately places teaching in the realm of information donation because it involves action directed at an immature. Unlike information donation, however, teaching requires *modified* directed action. As I interpret Caro and Hauser, if some behavior that is normally part of an adult's repertoire continues to be performed as always but is aimed specifically at an immature, it cannot count as teaching because no behavior was modified in the presence of the immature. It would count as information donation, in my terms.

Second, the teacher derives no benefit and may incur a cost as a result of its modified behavior. Although I have not set any requirements about costs or benefits for adults in information donation, this part of the definition would seem to apply to donation equally well. Any benefit to an adult from information donation would seem to come only in a delayed—not immediate—time frame, as is set forth in the definition of teaching. Similarly, it seems unnecessarily stringent to *require* the adult donor to incur a cost when, for example, its donation-related behavior might be a normal part of its repertoire.

Third, the pupil obtains some knowledge or skill as a result of the teaching. This requirement is likely to be a sticking point because in most studies, immatures haven't been followed intensively or long enough to evaluate changes in their skills or the source of any observed change (see, e.g., Caro and Hauser's discussion of the ontogeny of hunting skills in cheetahs). This problem is akin to that of assessing the strict requirements for social information transfer (and thus information donation): increased homogeneity of the social interactants' behavior over time. With teaching, as with information donation, specific hypotheses and measurements must be crafted as part of long-term studies to ensure that all components of strict definitions can be critically assessed.

Fourth, no criterion exists for intentionality on the part of the teacher. This aspect of the definition, which the authors admit sets them apart from most theorists, accords well with my criteria for information donation, in which directed action is defined without reference to intention.

The relationship, then, between teaching (if Caro and Hauser's definition is accepted) and information donation seems to be as follows: Meeting the criteria for teaching exceeds meeting those for information donation because the adult teacher—not the adult donor—must show modified behavior and because the pupil's changed behavior must occur as a direct result of the teaching behavior—whereas the recipient of information donation must show only increased homogeneity of behavior with the donor. When data are strong enough to point toward teaching, therefore, they can be counted as a type of information donation in which the directed action is also modified action.

My intent in this book is to distinguish and trace evolutionary changes between information acquisition and information donation, not to distinguish among various types of information donation. Teaching may, nonetheless, turn out to be an important category to bear in mind as the next chapters catalog examples of information donation. Caro and Hauser (1992:166) identify at least two mechanisms underlying teaching in nonhumans. In the first, the teacher puts the pupil in a situation conducive to learning a new skill, and in the second, the teacher alters the pupil's behavior directly through encouragement or punishment. When the data seem to indicate these types of teaching by nonhumans (even when, as with social information transfer, the exact definitional requirements may not be met), I use the term *teaching* to indicate a subtype of information donation that may be particularly important in tracing change over time in primate evolution.

Why, then, should social information transfer, either as teaching or in some other form, be used as the focus of a study? Simply put, it allows reliable measures of complex behaviors to be taken and meaningful conclusions to be drawn. Such conclusions include being able to say that information was transferred socially from adults to immatures and, more generally, that social interaction affected infant decision making. These conclusions may be more modest than those aimed for in a study of social learning, but I don't believe this is a significant problem because studies of social learning cannot address the complex issues. For anthropologists, social information transfer could become the concept of choice. Using it as the focal point of research avoids wasting time on unanswerable questions. It brings the focus back onto the effect that social interaction has on individuals. It can even play a role in strengthening links between studies of primate behavior and hominid behavior because, although there is no way to measure social learning in hominids, there are ways to measure social information transfer.

Primates and Primate Models

By now, it will be clear that the core of this book is based on data from primates, with comparisons made to hominids and modern humans. Year-long university courses and entire textbooks are devoted to questions of primate anatomy and behavior, and in a few pages I cannot do justice to either topic. Nevertheless, I want to present in summary form some highlights of the primate adaptation as a foundation for discussing social information transfer in primate species.

Descriptions and definitions of primates have abounded since the time of Linnaeus (reviewed by Conroy 1990). One of the most influential schemes was put forth by Clark (1959). In a break with the traditional approach, in which traits common to primates were simply listed, he identified a suite of evolutionary trends that together characterized the primate pattern (including that of humans). Three of these are "distinctive trends of the primate information system" (Jolly and Plog 1986:147).

First, for primates, the sense of vision dominates over the sense of smell. The reverse is true for most mammals. Primates process a great deal of visual information, and most primates have special adaptations for depth perception and color vision. Second, the primate hand is a remarkably dexterous organ that is capable of fine manipulation. Instead of feeding directly with the face, as other mammals do, primates use their hands to get food, process it, and bring it to the mouth. This manipulatory capacity is useful in a host of contexts other than foraging, including tool use.

Third, the primate brain is larger and more sophisticated than the brains of most other mammals. Monkeys and apes have bigger brains than any other land-living nonhuman mammals, once body-weight differences are held constant (Passingham 1982). Comparative measures of brain organization, as opposed to size, are more difficult to evaluate. The brains of a few primates seem to show some lateralization, meaning that the function of one hemisphere is not completely duplicated in the other as it is in most mammals—although only in humans does full lateralization occur (Passingham 1989). Gibson (1990) states straightforwardly that the human brain contains no significant unique structures and suggests that differences among mammalian brains are quantitative in much the same way that behaviors are.

In sum, the information-gathering and information-processing systems of primates differ from those of other mammals. Precise links between these anatomically based systems and actual behaviors are rarely understood, but it is known that in mammals, brain size and the connectivity patterns of neurons do strongly influence behavior (Gibson 1990). Thus it is not surprising that most ethologists consider primate behavior in at least some ways to be more sophisticated than the behavior of other animals, a position that accords well with the quantitative perspective taken here. With few exceptions, primates are social animals that live in groups, whether composed of tight-knit social units where membership changes only with demographic events or of communities with fluid comings and goings throughout each day. This intensely social environment, coupled with challenges from the physical environment, has evidently produced selection pressures for intelligence in primates (see chapter 5). Evidence exists that primates have the ability to distinguish kin from non-kin; they have knowledge of the relative positions of self and others in a dominance hierarchy that is often flexible and nonlinear; they share food and use and modify tools; they possess self-awareness; and they use deceptive and referential communication (see Cheney, Seyfarth, and Smuts 1986; Smuts et al. 1986).

At this point, I may seem to be veering dangerously close to primate chauvinism. Are primates really so special? After all, they make up an extremely small percentage of all animals on earth. Compare the number of species of primates—about two hundred—with that of beetles, about a quarter-million! All mammals taken together represent less than half of one percent of living animals (Voelker 1986). And primates make up only one of nineteen classes of mammals; others include carnivores, rodents, bats, and cetaceans. Many of these other mammals show sophisticated behaviors related to kin recognition and dominance, for example. Why then, as one zoologist I know is fond of asking, are primates alone, of all the mammalian classes, considered the subject of a distinct discipline? Why is there no International Society of Carnivorology?

Two kinds of answers to these questions can be offered. In the first place, the query about discipline boundaries is misleading. Before specializing in primates, a primatologist trains in a specific discipline, usually zoology, psychology, or anthropology. She must be familiar with entire subfields of knowledge within the larger discipline that are not directly related to primates or to her own research. In this she is no different from a zoologist who wishes to study lions but must train first in zoology, then specialize in mammalogy. The label *primatologist* designates not a narrow focus but rather a choice of theoretical context in which to carry out what may be a broadly based program of research.

Another possible response is less practical. Most anthropologists, many primatologists, and a good portion of the general public feel that the study of primates can shed more light on understanding ourselves and our ancestors than can the study of carnivores or bats. Why this should be the case is an interesting question; it may relate to the way humans seem fascinated most by the very animals from which they try hardest to set themselves apart. Nonetheless, for more than a century there has been good scientific justification for the belief that primates can inform us about human ancestors. Our common ancestor with other primates is more recent than that with other mammals, and our shared heritage in terms of things like brain size, brain organization, and intelligence is more pronounced. That primates are our closest relatives is not in dispute, but what use should be made of that fact is the subject of renewed debate.

Some anthropologists (Richard 1985; Foley 1987; DeVore 1990) now suggest that the traditional anthropological focus on primates as models for human ancestors is outdated. To these scholars, primates and hominids are first and foremost mammals, part of wider ecological communities. They should not, therefore, be seen as specialized beings climbing an evolutionary ladder toward humanity. It follows that only through study of ecology and community relationships will primatology succeed in shedding light on human behavior:

> Primatologists are on the threshold of developing a truly compara-
> tive socioecology. It is now possible to appreciate the irony that the
> emphasis on studies of our nearest primate relatives cannot alone
> explain why natural selection, over the last five million years, trans-
> formed the hominid lineage—why we are humans, and not chim-
> panzees or gorillas. Only as robust theory allows us to incorporate
> data from the farthest reaches of the animal kingdom are we likely to
> understand our own, unique adaptation. (DeVore 1990:4)

The view that primates can be profitably studied as mammals is a reason-able one. By studying all animals and not just our close relatives, broad ecologi-cal principles can be derived. Yet such an approach need not ignore the fact that primates are somehow "special" for those interested in human evolution. Studying the primates of today, of course, cannot answer every question about the process of becoming human, which took place gradually over millions of years. But doing so comes closer to identifying the selection pressures that affected hominids than does research on other species. Foley (1987) is right to point out that all animals are unique, and humans are just another unique species. Nonetheless, humans and other primates share more anatomical and behavioral traits than do humans and other animals. A focus on broad ecologi-cal communities need not replace one on primates as models for hominids if the models are carefully constructed.

Vital work continues to appear on primates as models for hominids (Kinzey 1987 and papers therein) or as a base for comparison with humans (Rodseth et al. 1991). Tooby and DeVore (1987:184) correctly claim that the question is not whether to use models but rather what kinds of models are most useful. Two types of models characterize the use of primates to understand hominids. Conceptual models are currently in fashion and, in general, are probably more worthwhile than referential models (Tooby and DeVore 1987; Harding 1991; but see McGrew 1992).

An underlying assumption of referential models is that one particular species of primate can be used as a living substitute for, or model of, a particular hominid or prehominid species. Baboons may be used to model australopithe-cines, for example, or chimpanzees may be used to model the common ances-tor shared by African great apes and hominids. Most primate models in the past have been of the referential type (e.g., DeVore and Washburn 1963; Tanner 1981, 1987), although confusion remains about what should be classified as referential and what as conceptual. Tanner, for example, focuses exclusively on the chimpanzee as a model for the creatures that lived immediately prior to the first hominids, but she claims that her model "is a conceptual framework" (1987:7). Most anthropologists would probably disagree. In any case, problems with referential models are myriad (see Tooby and DeVore 1987). A major one is that similarities between the model (say, chimpanzees) and its referent (say, prehominids) are emphasized over differences because, by definition, a referential model is set up to highlight similarities.

Conceptual models are meant to avoid this problem by analyzing relationships among sets of concepts or variables, not among tangible things or between extinct and living creatures. The underlying idea, as applied to primatology or any other study of living beings, is that

> species in the past were subject to the same fundamental evolutionary laws and ecological forces as species today, so that principles derived today are applicable throughout evolutionary history. Hence, each species is a unique expression of the same underlying principles: although no present species will correspond precisely to any past species, the principles that produced the characteristics of living species will correspond exactly to the principles that produced the characteristics of past species. (Tooby and DeVore 1987:190)

Conceptual models must focus not on the correspondence between two species separated in time but on principles and processes of evolutionary change. This is a tall order, and it is not surprising that within primatology few models measure up. An exception (see also Parker and Gibson 1979, discussed in chapter 5) is Strum and Mitchell's (1987) model focusing on behavioral shifts over time in a population of baboons. During her long-term study of African baboons, Strum observed some individuals begin rather suddenly to hunt small mammals, such as gazelles, in a sophisticated way. Male baboons carried out extended searches and cooperated with one another to chase down prey. This behavior differed greatly from the more casual, opportunistic approach toward potential prey seen in most baboon populations, including the one at Amboseli and Strum's study population itself before 1973.

The shift from opportunistic to sophisticated hunting apparently was a response to the rare co-occurrence of certain ecological, social, and psychological factors (Strum and Mitchell 1987:91, 96). Among these factors were the availability of prey of the right size and visibility for baboons; a scarcity of large predators that might inhibit the baboons' long-distance hunting (for baboons, safety is in numbers, and separation from the group often entails risk); and the presence of one baboon male who began the long-distance hunts and was copied by others in his group.

Strum and Mitchell make no claim that early hominids would at any point have acted exactly as Strum's baboons did. They do offer some interesting suggestions, however, that might apply to hominids. Individuals can play a critical role in initiating behavioral changes, and although ecological factors may be necessary, they may also be insufficient for initiation of a behavioral tradition. Thus, the emphasis is on process, resulting in a model less likely to be reductionistic than a referential model would be.

. In this book, I attempt to create neither a referential nor a conceptual model of the shifts in social information transfer over time. Although my field-work was done on baboons, I try not to emphasize them over other primates. I have no interest in formulating a referential model, and doing so would be difficult anyway, given my interest in incremental changes over the entire span of human evolution rather than in a particular species or time period. As for a conceptual model, it is simply premature to try to construct one when primatologists don't yet understand the variables that came into play in the evolution of communication in primates, much less how they co-occurred or interrelated.

In the spirit of some anthropologists (e.g., Rodseth et al. 1991), I try to use primates in a simpler way, as a baseline for comparison with hominids and humans. In a very real sense, though, this is a first step toward the eventual goal of building a conceptual model. Such a model would explain why hominids began to accumulate and donate information to immatures in more diverse and sophisticated ways than did primates. It would have to show how environmental, physiological, and social variables interrelated to kick off this change—or, more likely, the series of shifts involved in it.

Still, first steps must be taken before explanatory models can be constructed. The task at hand is to present and discuss the evidence for information donation and information acquisition among primates in certain contexts, and thus for the relative roles of adults and immatures in social information transfer.

2

THE SOCIAL BEHAVIOR OF MONKEYS AND APES

Although few behavioral patterns hold true for hundreds of species, one generalization can be made for almost all primates—they are highly group-oriented and social. The particular form the social unit takes and the degree of sociability within it do vary immensely, however, and this diversity forms the subject of a literature that is fascinating in its own right (e.g., Wrangham 1980; articles in Smuts et al. 1986). One way to discuss social structure is to consider briefly the variation first within monkeys and then within apes.

Among monkeys, at least one trait is shared by many Old and New World species. Individuals typically remain within sight or sound of other members of their immediate social unit, even during foraging, when individuals may be somewhat dispersed. Other than this trait, diversity is the rule. Social structure may be multimale and multifemale, or one male per social unit. Membership in the social unit may remain relatively constant over short periods of time, or smaller subgroups may combine into larger foraging or sleeping units at frequent and predictable intervals, perhaps daily.

Many of the best-studied monkey populations—including Old World cercopithecines such as savanna baboons, macaques, and vervets—tend to be multimale, multifemale, and matrilineal. In matrilineal groups, males transfer out at puberty to breed elsewhere, but females reproduce within their natal groups. Females thus grow up surrounded by kin from several generations—mothers, grandmothers, sisters, aunts, and so on—whereas males are typically without relatives in their breeding group. Mother-infant relationships are intense, sometimes nearly exclusive at birth. Female-female kin relationships are largely characterized by positive, friendly interactions. Individuals of both sexes, and indeed whole matrilines, may be ranked in dominance hierarchies; males are usually dominant over females.

Not all Old World monkeys, of course, fit these patterns. Some species, including the colobines such as the langur monkey, live (most often, although not exclusively) in one-male groups where dominance among females may be influenced by age but is weakly expressed when compared to the dominance hierarchies of baboons or macaques. Many females may participate in the care-taking of individual infants among langurs and similar species. Cercopithecines and colobines thus differ in some significant ways, but great diversity can be found even by comparing closely related cercopithecines living in one-male units, as Stammbach (1986) shows by examining forest, desert, and mountain baboons.

As Strier (1990) has pointed out, New World monkeys differ in many ways from the better-studied Old World species. Dispersal at puberty is one important difference: "The occurrence of female transfer in the majority of Anthropoid genera also suggests that most female primates do not live in kin groups, as is generally assumed" (Strier 1990:16). Other behavioral differences involve dominance between the sexes and competition for resources; in Brazilian muriquis (woolly spider monkeys), for example, females are codominant with males, or sometimes dominant over them.

Diversity of social structure seems even more pronounced among apes than among monkeys, if only because there are so few species of apes. Primates classified as apes, all located in the Old World, include the so-called lesser apes of Asia—the gibbon and siamang (with a monogamous, family social structure). One of the four great apes is from Asia as well—the orangutan (often solitary, except for mothers with dependent offspring, and during mating). The other great apes are African—the gorilla (usually found in one-male groups), the bonobo, and the chimpanzee (both found in multimale, multifemale communities, although association patterns between them differ).

Social units of monkeys and apes, even when tightly cohesive, are neither closed nor static. Immigration and emigration (as well as birth and death) cause demographic changes over time, and large groups may fission permanently. In some cases, changes in association patterns occur as part of a daily rhythm: for example, when smaller social units combine into bigger ones during foraging or for sleeping at night. When the social unit is not tightly cohesive—as in the cases of the chimpanzee and the New World spider monkey, which live in fission-fusion societies—the composition of subgroups changes even more frequently. In such cases, the individual is faced with what amounts to frequent, short-term demographic changes.

As Goodall (1986:147) remarks, a chimpanzee "rarely sees all the members of his community on the same day and probably never sees them two days in succession." This situation differs radically from that of the more stable social unit characteristic of most primates. In fact, although they are usually thought of as exceptionally social, chimpanzees, especially females, may spend quite a large portion of the day alone or with close kin only. Females are dispersed in individual territories through which others may roam. Goodall's data (1986:168–69) for seven females show that time spent alone, or with family only, accounted for the majority of time each day that the chimpanzees were observed. For the remainder of a chimpanzee female's day, she encounters other community members in shifting (but not random) patterns of association. The chimpanzee form of sociability thus may be more "complicated" than the cohesive social units of most monkeys, at least to the extent that constantly shifting association patterns mean more information must be processed and more variables taken into account than in a group of relatively constant membership.

Two points relevant to an understanding of information transfer emerge from this brief review. First, primates are committed to sociability, and acquiring social skills is thus critical for each individual. In order to negotiate life within its group and to mate and reproduce successfully there or elsewhere, an immature primate must acquire a host of social skills. Doing so depends, in turn, on acquiring information. Second, primate social life is organized around kinship and dominance, both of which are highly significant influences on an individual's social experience (Cheney, Seyfarth, and Smuts 1986). A monkey or ape surrounded by relatives, for example, is likely to have a very different life than one isolated from its kin. Many primatologists (see Gouzoules and Gouzoules 1986; Bernstein 1991) have discovered that when an individual primate has relatives nearby, its social support and affiliative interactions often increase, as does its access to other resources. Similar differences sometimes correlate with dominance rank (Silk 1986).

For a primate, then, many social skills related to kinship and to the social unit's dominance system, if any, must be acquired, especially during the infant and juvenile periods. The relative ranking of individuals within dominance hierarchies shifts over time, and because of demographic changes within the social group, so does the availability of an individual's kin. As a result, an individual's position in the group changes, requiring an ability to understand both the situation at any given moment and alterations that occur in it.

My aim in this chapter is to consider the relative roles of adults and infants in the processes by which immatures acquire information about social skills. I include in the chapter the subject of social information transfer concerning predator avoidance—on the face of it, a seemingly arbitrary choice, since such behavior is no more inherently social than the foraging and tool-use behaviors treated in the next chapter. I hope to show, however, that social skills and predator behavior can be separated from foraging and tool use (at least hypothetically), based on certain features of social information transfer.

27

Socialization

That most primates are social does not mean that acquiring social skills comes rapidly or easily. The process is a gradual one, influenced by all the variables just discussed and many more. The individualistic nature of attaining social skills for all animals has been emphasized by Mason (1979:1):

> Becoming social is a matter of individual history—part of the un-ending dialogue between the organism and its environment that is characteristic of all life processes. More than that, it is the development of competencies and skills, of deficiencies and aberrations, the realization of potentials whose nature can be discerned only after the fact.

Typically, the ways in which immature primates acquire social skills are lumped under the umbrella term *socialization,* a word that has been used so frequently and so variously that it now means vastly different things to different people. According to Swartz and Rosenblum (1981:417), the term most often has referred to "the influence of a diversity of social, biological and maturational factors over time that ultimately result in an appropriately functioning adult who is capable of interacting in a species-typical and predictable fashion with other members of its species."

This description accurately captures a key feature of the traditional view of primate socialization—that it is "adultcentric" (see Peters n.d.). That is, the focus is on the final product, the adult (indeed, an "appropriately functioning adult"). Adult behavior is taken as the norm; usually, infant and juvenile behavior is tracked over time and compared at each stage to adult behavior. Observing the gradual conformity of the two is often the goal of socialization studies, which have a strong interest in discovering how adults shape the development of their young. The mother is usually the primary agent of socialization, according to this view.

Such a perspective has validity and merit. No figure is more important in the life of a primate infant than its mother; shortly after birth, a mother and her infant may seem to constitute a single unit, so tight is their association (Rowell 1975). The mother does shape the infant's social world. At its earliest ages, for instance, the infant associates with the same individuals the mother associates with. Examples of adult influence, direct and otherwise, on infant development are discussed later—after all, information donation by adults is one of this chapter's themes.

Nevertheless, the typical view of socialization is too narrow. It ignores or underemphasizes both the active role taken by the infant in its own and others' social life, and the possibility of adaptive, age-specific behavior in immatures. Fortunately, an atypical approach to socialization has been adopted by some ethologists, primatologists, and anthropologists (e.g., Rowell 1975; Trivers 1985; Baldwin 1986; Fairbanks 1988; Dolhinow 1991; Owings 1994; Peters 1994) who base their conceptual or empirical research on the belief that infants may be studied as more than adults waiting to unfold. A focus on age-specific behavior, for example, may allow for the possibility that immature behavior differs from adult behavior not only because immatures make mistakes as they gradually conform to an adult norm but also because different solutions may be more effective for infants than for adults. When an infant behaves differently from an adult, it is worth considering that it may have a good reason for doing so.

Almost 20 years ago, Rowell noted that the label *socialization* implies "a process applied 'from above' by older animals to originally asocial infants until they conform to some standard known as 'adulthood' " (1975:126). As she and others have pointed out, the behavioral interaction in socialization is actually two way. Immatures often affect the experiences and behavior of their older groupmates. Behavioral innovation, such as incorporation of new foods into the diet, is a good example because it most often is originated by juveniles (Nishida 1986). From juveniles, the behavior may then be passed on to other group members, altering species-typical diet. Another fascinating example—and one more in accord with social skills as envisioned in this chapter—comes from research on the langur monkey.

Caretaking of infants in the common Indian langur monkey (*Presbytis entellus*) is not characterized by the intense, near-exclusive bond between mother and infant found in the matrilineal macaques and baboons. Langur mothers and infants are bonded, of course, but a system of multiple-female caretaking operates in which infants are not the exclusive social property of their mothers (McKenna 1981:395). Rather, by the time they are only a few months old, langur infants accumulate social experience with a diversity of adult females who vary in age and maternal experience and who include "an extraordinary array of personality types" (McKenna 1981:395).

The implications of this pattern for social information transfer in langurs, compared to some other monkeys, are interesting. Langur infants, it would seem, have more opportunities at an earlier age to acquire information from a variety of animals with different individual experiences of the world than do monkeys whose infants are exclusively bonded to their mothers. A hypothesis worth testing would be that monkeys, including langurs, with a multiple-caretaking system acquire information more rapidly (at earlier ages), or acquire more diverse information, than do primates with more intense mother-infant bonds.

The aspect of this system that I wish to concentrate on, however, is adoption, for it illustrates how the infant can play an active role in its own socialization and how, in doing so, it can affect the social lives of others around it.

Adoption (and a wide array of other behaviors) in langurs has been studied by Dolhinow and her colleagues (e.g., Dolhinow and DeMay 1982; Dolhinow and Murphy 1982). Dolhinow's view of the active primate infant can be summarized as follows:

> Popular accounts of immaturity, especially those focusing on the very young, tend to stress dependency and helplessness. The "needy" infant receives attention and care; and although it is usually credited with participation in the relation that builds between it and its mother, it is seldom portrayed as an active and often skillful, persistent, opportunistic manipulator of its social world. Immaturity usually is also considered to be a time of preparation for maturity. . . . Knowledge and skills are carried forward and consolidated as a primate ages, but emphasizing early years as mainly preparation for the future may detract from a full appreciation of how the immature survives, first as an infant and later as a juvenile. . . . The infant needs to be skilled in what it does, from day one. (Dolhinow 1991:139)

Langur adoption, at least in the captive colony in which Dolhinow did her research, is a showcase for the early appearance of infants' social skills. Adoption, usually conceived in human-oriented terms as an adult's actively choosing to adopt a passive infant, can better be defined as transfer of infant attachment from the mother to another adult female (Dolhinow and DeMay 1982). It may take place in the enforced absence of the mother, when she dies or is removed from the group by researchers, or in her presence—for example, at weaning. Among Dolhinow's langurs, adoption is initiated by the infant, who takes responsibility for seeking out a particular female caretaker and maintaining proximity and contact with her. Some infants are quite persistent in these behaviors. They clearly alter their own activities to minimize interference with the potential adopter's activities, thus increasing their chances of gaining proximity or contact with the targeted female. Interestingly, kinship is not a factor in an infant's choice of caretakers. Infants are not always successful; some are rejected by their chosen caretakers. Whatever the outcome, infants are often active participants in their own socialization and at the same time in others' lives.

Dolhinow's description of primate infants as "opportunistic manipulators" echoes theoretical predictions from the field of sociobiology. As Trivers (e.g., 1974, 1985) originally pointed out, parental investment in an infant benefits that infant but costs the parent(s) in terms of lifetime reproductive potential. At some point, then, the parent should substantially decrease its investment in a given infant in order to invest elsewhere. The infant, meanwhile, should "want" high levels of investment to be maintained. That the same interaction carries different costs and benefits for parent and child is the foundation for Trivers's insight that "from an early age the offspring is expected to be a psychologically sophisticated creature. The offspring should be able to evaluate the cost of parental actions and their benefits. When the offspring's interests diverge from those of its parents, the offspring is selected to employ a series of psychological maneuvers" (1985:158). Throwing a tantrum during weaning might be an example of such a maneuver.

In short, from the vantage point of information acquisition and donation, socialization is a complex, two-way process. Adults may direct attention to key places, events, or conspecifics in an infant's life, and thus affect infant behavior even in the absence of true information donation. Or adults may actively donate information in the various ways outlined in this book. Infants may help shape their own socialization and also social information transfer via active information acquisition. The main task of the rest of this chapter is to discuss the relative roles of immatures and adults in social information transfer about social skills and predator avoidance.

Acquiring Social Skills

Do mothers or other adults actually donate information about social skills to immatures? Most studies of adult-infant interactions allow only the conclusion that the mother's behavior (or the behavior of adult males, siblings, etc.) is a strong influence on the composition of the infant's social world and on its socialization. This view is reinforced by observations of orphaned animals in the wild and by captive "separation studies" where infants are deprived of normal maternal contact in some way.

Among the best studies of the mother's effect on an infant's early social associations are Berman's (e.g., 1982a, 1982b) on free-ranging rhesus monkeys (*Macaca mulatta*) at Cayo Santiago, an island off Puerto Rico. Unlike langurs, rhesus monkeys do not exhibit caretaking by multiple adult females. The mother-infant bond in rhesus monkeys is intense and embedded in a matrilineal network. In the Cayo Santiago population, the infant's social network mirrors its mother's not only shortly after birth but also as late as 30 weeks of age. This prolonged dependence suggests the possibility that maternal behavior has long-term consequences for the development of the infant's social networks in rhesus monkeys (Berman 1982a, 1982b), and probably in other monkeys with this type of social organization.

Berman does not describe the maternal role as an active one in which the mother directly intervenes to promote certain social relationships and discourage others. She does note, however, some intriguing maternal behaviors in rhesus monkeys and other cercopithecines that may approach active guidance. By reacting to other group members with fear, intolerance, or attraction, some mothers provide "differential cues" (Berman, personal communication), both to their infants and to potential interactants, about their arousal states or about the potential outcomes of certain interactions. Rhesus mothers, for instance, sometimes prevent interaction between their infants and other group members by grabbing the infants and distracting them, or by threatening the other monkeys (Berman, personal communication).

De Waal's (1990) observations on a captive colony augment the suggestion of subtle but active interference by rhesus mothers, who sometimes execute what de Waal terms "double-holds": a mother picks up another female's infant and clasps it to her body along with her own infant. The most remarkable aspect of this behavior is that infants to be held were chosen selectively, the preferred infants belonging to high-ranking females. As de Waal notes, a possible explanation for this preference is that rhesus females know which mother each infant belongs to, and by targeting high-ranking infants they are selectively promoting beneficial future bonds for their own infants. This possibility, although only one alternative, is not farfetched; good evidence exists to show that monkey mothers know to whom infants belong.

If hypothesis testing confirms this explanation, double-hold maternal behavior may be an excellent example of active intervention in which mothers guide infants in how best to select social companions. Because mothers modify their normal behavior in the presence of infants and presumably derive no immediate benefit of their own from double-holds, this behavior may qualify as the type of teaching in which adults put immatures in situations conducive to learning (Caro and Hauser 1992).

Two conclusions about the extent of information donation for social skills in primates emerge from a general literature review. First, curiously enough, few systematic explorations of the topic have been carried out, and no one, to my knowledge, has synthesized the data that are available. Second, adults do intervene in immatures' social interactions, although descriptions of such interventions do not always reveal cases of information donation. As a general rule, primate adults monitor and respond to their offspring when the offspring are involved in social situations, especially when the situations are, or might become, threatening. Mothers may be vigilant as their offspring approach other group members and may punish others (immatures and adults alike) who threaten or play too roughly with their offspring. This type of behavior has been aptly described by Chism (1991:104), who has studied African patas monkeys:

> For most of the first year, monkey mothers actively intervene in encounters involving their infants, threatening other animals that are aggressive to their infants and even chasing off lower ranking animals

that are attempting friendly interactions. As infants spend increasing amounts of time out of their mothers' immediate proximity, they
must assume more and more responsibility for their own social interactions.

Judging from accounts in the field and in captivity, this kind of active intervention is common in apes as well as monkeys. In matrilineal species, intervention may be carried out by a variety of relatives other than the mother; kinship
is a reliable predictor of who comes to an immature's aid. In many species,
threats or actual interventions by the mother and other adult female kin play
a significant role in the acquisition of rank within the female dominance hierarchy (Walters 1986:311). Clearly, though, this type of intervention does not
amount to information donation. The mother or other relative essentially pro-
tects her infant, rescues it from harm, and punishes others. Information may
be transferred, through threat, chase, or actual punishment, to other animals
about the consequences of treating a particular infant in a particular way. The
infant itself may well attend to and acquire information from such encounters,
thus engaging in information acquisition as defined in chapter 1.

For information donation to take place *to the immature,* however, some
action or signal must be directed at it—for example, through discouragement (punishment) or encouragement. Cheney and Seyfarth (1990:224–25)
claim that

> the most common approximation to teaching in free-ranging mon-
> keys and apes occurs in the form of punishment for some social trans-
> gression. Mothers aggressively interfere in rough play between their
> offspring and other juveniles, retrieve their infants from females who
> are handling them roughly, push infants from their nipples during the
> weaning period, and so on. These corrective actions, however, occur
> primarily as threats, and they seem to derive less from pedagogical
> intent than from an attempt by others to remedy what is aversive or
> unpleasant to *themselves.* . . . To the extent that they correct others,
> they seem to be attempting to make others behave in a way that is
> beneficial to themselves.

Several comments about Cheney and Seyfarth's statements come to mind.
First, to the extent that the behaviors described involve immediate benefits
for the mother, they do not match the definition of teaching I am using in this
book. Second, I construe maternal intent, or the motivation for mothers' intervention—whether tied to self-interest or not—as beside the point for deciding
whether teaching or other forms of information donation are taking place. For

33

information donation to occur, there need be no demonstration that mothers intend to transfer information to the immature, but only that they direct to immatures some action that results in information transfer. Third, in Cheney and Seyfarth's two examples involving social skills, it remains unclear whether it is the infant or other group members that are punished. Retrieving infants or intervening in rough play may in some cases be aversive enough to the infant to constitute punishment. Alternatively, it may be mild enough to be experienced by the infant as direction rather than the punishment it sometimes experiences in the form of maternal biting or hitting during weaning (e.g., J. Altmann 1980:175).

This fine point aside, it is clear that primate mothers do sometimes guide or punish their infants in social situations. When a chimpanzee infant toddles up to an adult male, the mother may permit the ensuing contact, or, alternatively, she may hurriedly retrieve the infant. The maternal response seems determined by the male's reaction to the infant—for example, whether he shows piloerection or other signs of arousal at the infant's approach or touch (Goodall 1986). In this way, the infant may acquire from its mother information about how to read conspecifics' social signals, when to pursue and when to abandon social interactions, and so on. Finally, if, despite these comments, Cheney and Seyfarth are correct in their claim that punishment is the best example of information donation in primates, their conclusion still supports the overall thesis of this book, that information donation occurs in few contexts, and rarely, in primates.

Some mother monkeys do guide the development of locomotion skills in their infants (Hinde and Simpson 1975; J. Altmann 1980:130; Milton 1988: 292). Milton's description of maternal guidance of infant locomotion among spider monkeys in Panama is worth reading in detail:

> [Female] spider monkeys spend time with their young offspring carrying out behaviours that appear to teach immature animals how to travel alone along foraging routes. A female spider monkey will begin to move along a foraging route, but will then sit down. Eventually, her infant grows tired of waiting and moves forward away from her a short distance through the trees along the route. The mother will then get up and move along behind the infant, reinforcing its independent locomotion through the trees in the position of leader, not follower. This can be a time-consuming process. It requires what a human observer would describe as considerable patience on the part of the mother, who, being hungry, should prefer to move rapidly to food trees rather than sit for many minutes waiting for her offspring to take the travelling initiative.

This observation and the few others like it suggest, as does direction or punishment of infants' social behavior, that some monkeys and apes show the capacity for information donation, probably via teaching in some cases. Yet despite the thousands of hours scientists have spent studying socialization in primates, few instances of information donation regarding social skills are known. Perhaps information donation occurs in subtle ways to which primatologists have rarely been attuned. From what is currently known, though, it appears that immatures acquire information about social skills mostly on their own.

Play and observational learning are the ways most often cited by which immatures could acquire the information needed to adopt the social behavior expected of them. For example, play allows practice of skills directly related to competing for resources. Experience obtained from direct interaction with conspecifics, however, may not always be necessary for figuring out where one fits into a particular dominance hierarchy. Among some primates, infants learn their relative dominance rank very early in life, before they are able to participate directly in dominance-related interactions. This is possible because their rank is tied in a predictable way to their mother's rank, and because they observe dominance relationships between their mother and others, or between other conspecifics (e.g., Cheney 1977). Information acquisition, therefore, occurs even at these early ages. Participation and intervention by female kin are important, but information donation in a strict sense seems absent.

As a comprehensive view of socialization would predict, immatures may do more than play and watch the behavior of their groupmates; they may also set up their own social experiences in particular ways. Juvenile baboons in Amboseli, Kenya, appear to be attracted to same-sex older conspecifics, so that "juveniles create opportunities to observe and learn sex-specific behaviour by selectively associating with same-sex adults" (Pereira 1988:200). Juvenile females were more attracted to adult females than were juvenile males, who preferred to associate with adolescent and adult males. Additional selectivity beyond same-sex association was also found by Pereira. Juvenile females, for example, associated more often with older kin than did juvenile males, who associated at comparable rates with related and unrelated adult females. This difference makes sense because female baboons at Amboseli stay in their natal group to breed, and would benefit greatly from kin-based support, whereas most males transfer out to breed in another group.

Information acquisition by immatures in the social arena is a neglected research topic. Maternal-infant separation studies show that social input is needed for healthy development of social skills, but few studies (except those devoted to observational learning) have been aimed at demonstrating precisely how an infant makes use of being near, or interacting with, older conspecifics.

Vocal-Auditory Referential Communication in Acquiring Social Skills

How else, other than by direct behavioral intervention and discouragement, might primate adults donate information to immatures about social skills? Research on primate vocal communication, especially referential communication, hints that information donation might be accomplished through vocal production or as a result of incoming vocal signals. Although few firm conclusions can be drawn, some intriguing cases highlight the possible relationship between referential vocal communication and information acquisition and donation.

The ability of some primates to communicate referentially—that is, about specific features of the environment rather than just about emotion—was mentioned in chapter 1. Conspecifics, of course, are "specific features of the environment" just as much as are fruiting trees or dangerous predators. Referential communication has been discovered—at least arguably (see Snowdon 1990)—in several behavioral contexts in primates, including not only social relationships and predator avoidance but also foraging. The best evidence for referential communication comes from playback experiments, which allow scientists to find out what kinds of categories are used by, and are meaningful for, the animals themselves.

The playback procedure (see Cheney and Seyfarth 1990 for details) is to tape-record vocalizations that occur in some natural context, perhaps an aggressive interaction between two females or a predator's approaching the group. Later, in the absence of the stimulus (the interaction or the predator), the vocalizations are played back to the animals. If the subjects react in predictable, consistent ways over many trials, it shows that the vocalizations themselves encode some type of specific information about the environment and not just about an animal's arousal state. They would thus constitute referential communication. The playback experiment effectively controls for other sources of information that might ordinarily be available to the listener, such as the caller's face, body, and posture. The channels over which information can be carried are thus limited by the technique, allowing a research focus on the vocal-auditory channel.

Playback experiments allow innovative research into cognition and communication, but they are not flawless. For one thing, they cannot indicate the relative contributions of emotion and reference in any vocalization. Referential calls may contain an emotional component and may give information about the caller's subsequent behavior (Cheney and Seyfarth 1990). This is neither surprising nor bothersome to those whose goal is only to demonstrate empirically that primates are capable of expressing more than emotion. A more significant concern is expressed by Snowdon (1992:167–68), who points out that the playback technique is powerful for demonstrating an animal's ability to respond to the information coded in a signal in the absence of any other context features, but it reveals little about the cognitive abilities of the caller itself. These limitations are now widely recognized, but most scholars interested in the evolution of communication agree that despite them, the playback approach provides fascinating new perspectives.

Cheney and Seyfarth, for example, used results from playback experiments on primates as the basis for their conclusion that "concepts like kinship and dominance rank, devised by humans to explain what monkeys do, exist not only in the minds of human observers but also in the minds of their subjects" (1990:122). Such a view is enormously reassuring to primatologists, who have long hoped that they were not simply imposing a classificatory system for kinship and dominance onto their subjects. Three examples of referential communication in monkeys, as studied using the playback technique, will indicate the types of vocal abilities discovered so far, and which may play a role in social information transfer.

Among the Cayo Santiago rhesus monkeys, the same population studied by Berman in her research on mother-infant association patterns, immature monkeys use referential communication to indicate certain features of behavioral interactions. When under threat or attack from adults, they give five different kinds of screams, each significantly associated with two external referents: type of opponent, defined in terms of dominance rank and matrilineal relatedness to the signaler; and severity of the aggression, differentiated as to whether or not physical contact occurred (Gouzoules, Gouzoules, and Marler 1984). The five types of screams are given, respectively, during interactions with higher-ranking opponents with either high or low probability of physical contact, with lower-ranking opponents without physical contact, and (for two types) with matrilineal relatives.

After reviewing and rejecting possible alternatives, Snowdon (1990) concludes that these screams are a good example of representational signals. I agree, especially because the screams did not intergrade with each other, as would be expected if they indicated the relative intensity of the immature's fear. Note that in this case the information is transferred from immatures to adults rather than the other way around, so it does not meet the criterion for information donation.

What does makes this case relevant for understanding information donation from adults to immatures is that adult rhesus monkeys respond differentially according to scream type. When immatures scream during interactions with relatives, mothers respond for shorter periods and after longer delays than they do for screams involving nonrelatives, indicating less concern for interactions in which relatives are their offspring's opponents. The problem for deciding whether this behavior counts as information donation is that the response in this experiment, as in many other playback experiments, was not measured in direct action but simply by whether or not the subjects looked in the direction of the speaker used during playback (Gouzoules, Gouzoules, and Marler 1984:189).

Apparently mothers do not perceive aggression from relatives as a threat equal to one from a member of some other matriline—a distinction that seems logical given that their own positions in the group may be affected by aggression from outside their matriline (Marler 1985). Whether mothers' differential responses are motivated by self-interest or not, they would constitute information donation if they were coupled with active intervention and thus guidance about the development of relationships with group members of various types, and about which interactions were most threatening to immatures. A similar system of screams was found in another macaque species, the pigtail macaque (*M. nemestrina*; Gouzoules and Gouzoules 1989). The rhesus example, then, is not an isolated one, and comparative research across species may be carried out.

Vervets (*Cercopithecus aethiops*), another African monkey with a matrilineal social system, also use referential communication in the context of social relationships. Vervets at Amboseli, Kenya, utter grunt vocalizations in four different situations: when approaching a dominant monkey, when approaching a subordinate, when initiating group movement across an open plain, and when sighting another vervet group (Struhsaker 1967; Cheney and Seyfarth 1982, 1990). Cheney and Seyfarth carried out playback experiments so that one vervet's grunts were recorded in each of the four contexts and then played back in a paired-comparison design. For example, grunts originally given toward a dominant animal and grunts originally given to another group were paired in testing (although played back several days apart). Unless grunts contained specific information about the social environment, Cheney and Seyfarth reasoned, responses to these two types of grunts should be the same. They were not; responses differed according to grunt type even when the context varied in which it was played back. Upon hearing grunts to a dominant, vervets looked at the loudspeaker, but upon hearing grunts to another group, vervets looked off across the savanna, in the direction in which the loudspeaker was pointed. These and similar results in other experiments strongly suggest that vervet grunts encode specific information.

According to Cheney and Seyfarth's data, grunts directed toward animals of a rank different from the caller's serve to further certain social interactions: they increase the probability that animals of different ranks will forage, feed, or sit together. Grunts made at the start of movement across the savanna may decrease the risk of predation by heightening group members' attention, and grunts directed to another group probably serve as notification that the first group is already in the area (Cheney and Seyfarth 1990:119). At least some of the grunts may be significant sources of information for immatures who attend to them. As in the rhesus example, until it is shown that adults direct their grunts, or responses to them, toward immatures, no claim for information donation can be made.

Vocal referential communication exists for New World as well as Old World monkeys (Snowdon 1990). Captive cotton-top tamarins (*Saguinus o. oedipus*), for instance, give two variants of their chirp call. One variant is given during territorial encounters, when the sounds of an unfamiliar group are heard. When other tamarins hear this chirp, they show increased activity, freezing, scanning, and piloerection, and they utter more of a certain vocalization related to high arousal. The second variant is given as a contact call in nonthreatening situations and does not result in the same behavioral changes. When the two variants were played back to tamarins, the monkeys discriminated between them—that is, responded in the ways appropriate to each—even though the calls were only 75 milliseconds in duration and had very similar acoustic structures. Here again, immatures may get information from the chirp calls of adults; whether calls given in the wild, or responses to them, are directed at immatures is not known.

Two general conclusions about the vocalization systems of rhesus, vervet, and tamarin monkeys can be offered. First, they constitute referential communication. Second, immatures can get and/or give a great deal of useful information about the social environment using referential calls. The key question, as yet unanswered, is this: Do these vocalizations function in information donation from adults to immatures? Because various calls encode specific information about the social environment, it is likely that information is transferred from adults to immatures. But for information donation to be operating, the messages or responses to them must be aimed specifically at immatures (or other inexperienced individuals). The hypothesis that the calls themselves constitute information donation must be tested by measuring whether the calls increase in the presence (or decrease in the absence) of immatures or in situations where immatures are particularly vulnerable.

In short, no strong support is yet available for the suggestion that referential vocal communication in primates acts as information donation. Of course, I have considered only three examples, but they seem to be representative of the few that are known. This entire area of research—everything encompassed by referential communication and information donation—is in its infancy. Hypothesis testing about the interpretation of referential vocal communication as information donation seems promising. Research is needed on all primate species, but especially apes.

My choice of three examples of referential vocalizations from monkeys alone is not random: research on vocal communication in apes has lagged behind that for monkeys. Playback experiments have not been reported for apes; such reports would fill a real gap in the primatological data. Ape communication may depend more on facial expression and gesture than on vocal communication (Snowdon 1990), although this conclusion may be premature considering how few experiments have been done akin to those carried out for other species. The topic of referential vocal communication, with data once again coming mostly from monkeys, will be revisited later in the discussion of predator avoidance.

Meanwhile, what of the active primate infant? It should now be evident that a simple dichotomy between adult- and infant-mediated social information transfer is, in actual application, rather too simple. The examples just given, although intended to highlight adult roles, themselves offer clues about the role played by infants. In the rhesus example, it is the screams of immatures, not the vocalizations of adults, that are referential. In the other cases, if adults do not use referential vocal signals specifically to donate information to immatures, then two alternatives come to mind: either immatures don't make use of the information contained in the calls, or they pay attention and use the information even though it is not aimed specifically at them. Based on what we know of primate infants, the second option is more likely.

Few research projects on primate vocal communication have embraced a research design sensitive to emotional versus referential communication. Primates, of course, use vocal communication in a multitude of ways, many of them related to social behavior; we simply do not know how much of this vocal behavior is referential. Most studies to date have aimed at understanding the functions of various calls, or at least the behavioral consequences stemming from them. The functions (using the term in a casual sense) of primate vocalizations range from attracting mates and promoting group cohesion to maintaining distance among rivals. Readers interested in the diversity of primate vocal behavior should consult more comprehensive sources (S. Altmann 1967; Snowdon, Brown, and Petersen 1982; Seyfarth 1986).

The complexity of primate vocal communication, and the potential role it plays it social information transfer, can be illustrated by the vocalizations of white-cheeked gibbons (*Hylobates concolor leucogenys*), a monogamous lesser ape of Asia. Mated pairs of this species sing carefully coordinated duets that advertise their bonded status; their offspring may vocalize as well, although not as part of the duet. Deputte's (1982:87) description of gibbon vocal behavior shows that it may well be implicated in social information transfer:

The white-cheeked gibbon duet is more than a mere female plus male song. It appears to signal the existence and location of a still-established mating pair. The duet, in gibbons, seems to act to protect the monogamous structure. Nonmated females surrounding a duetting pair are informed of the presence of a mated female and are likely to be maintained at a distance by the aggressive components of the female song. They are also informed that the male in the vicinity is already mated, because of the precise, temporally adjusted response to *his* female partner's song. In addition, the chorus of the juveniles may transmit a message about the size of the family group and perhaps even its socionomic composition.

Deputte (1982) suggests that gibbon vocalizations have both intergroup and intragroup functions: to promote intergroup spacing and intragroup cohesion, respectively. In gibbons, according to the presence or absence of songs and song type, some unmated animals may receive information about where mating opportunities are, and are not, likely to be found. As with many other examples cited here, it can safely be concluded that immatures may attend to gibbon duets and other calls and acquire information from them; evidence for information donation awaits more research.

To summarize about social skills: the best evidence for information donation related to social skills comes from the guidance of immatures' social behavior through direction or discouragement—but even here, data are relatively scarce. To date, the best interpretation of the evidence suggests that much information about social skills and social behavior is available to immatures from adults, but that adults rarely donate information specifically to them. The alternative explanation—that primatologists, conditioned by received wisdom not to expect guidance or teaching in primates, have not yet tested the appropriate hypotheses or noticed and reported the appropriate anecdotes—must be borne in mind.

Acquiring Predator-Avoidance Skills

All the social skills in the world will not help a primate survive and reproduce if it cannot avoid being eaten by another animal. Predator avoidance is thus another area in which social information transfer may be expected to be important for primates, especially monkeys. As of 1986, no successful predation on an ape had been recorded in a long-term study (Cheney and Wrangham 1986:231).

The degree to which predation pressure influences primate behavior is largely unknown, but predation has significant demographic impact on at least some monkey populations (Cheney and Wrangham 1986, especially table 1). A good example is the Amboseli vervet population, where 70 percent of all deaths are thought to be caused by predation on healthy animals. Mortality due to predators is not, of course, perfectly correlated with predation pressure; antipredator behavior may be strongly selected for in populations where deaths from predation are relatively few, and may explain the low rate.

Generalizing about predation across primate species is as difficult as it is with other topics. Among some identifiable patterns are these: carnivores and raptors are the most common predators on primates, with terrestrial primates more vulnerable to the first and arboreal primates more vulnerable to the second; no consistent differences are seen in predation rates according to social structure, that is, multimale versus one-male groups; and predator-avoidance strategies include a diversity of behaviors, such as concealment, vigilance, flight, and attack (Cheney and Wrangham 1986).

Referential vocal communication in predator avoidance has been well studied in some species. Experimental studies with a specific focus on antipredator vocal communication will be discussed later. First, I will consider reports of antipredator behavior in both wild and captive monkeys and apes.

Among wild Peruvian squirrel monkeys (*Saimiri oerstedi*), adults warn infants to avoid both predators and noxious prey species (Boinski and Fragaszy 1989). The latter category includes caterpillars that may be toxic if not processed carefully before ingestion. An anecdote included in this report provides a rare glimpse of information donation in wild primates. On one particular day

> the majority of the troop used the same branch to cross a forest gap. An 8-cm-long black saturnyid caterpillar lay unobscured on a leaf adjacent to the travel path. At least eight adults came to a full stop in front of the leaf bearing the caterpillar before continuing. When a group of four infants also paused by the caterpillar an adult male returned, gave several bark vocalizations, and placed himself between the infants and the caterpillar. The infants then looked closely at the caterpillar again before continuing. (Boinski and Fragaszy 1989:423)

The caterpillar in this example is not strictly a predator, but the same interventions and bark vocalizations were made by adult monkeys when other potentially dangerous animals, including opposums, snakes, and owls, were encountered. No details of these interactions are given in the published report. Nonetheless, it is clear that the behavior of adults in this population goes beyond protective responses in which the infant is retrieved or rescued once it is already in harm's way (although under the right circumstances, such direction of action, too, might count as information donation). Adult squirrel monkeys donate information to immatures about predator avoidance through intervention and vocal warnings—modified behaviors directed at the immatures in a way that strongly suggests teaching.

Intriguing hints of information donation are reported for Peruvian tamarins

(*Saguinus fuscicollis*). During the play sessions of young monkeys, adults position themselves "on different sides of the playing offspring, as if they were being especially alert for predators that could be attracted by the raucous young" (Goldizen 1986:37). Observation of adult behavior once a predator actually appears, whether or not it threatens the playing young, would indicate whether information donation or only protective behavior occurs in this tamarin population.

Predators, especially snakes, may be "mobbed" by primates. According to my own observations of Amboseli baboons and descriptions from studies of other species, members of a social group may approach or even attack a snake, rather than fleeing from it. Snake mobbing was observed among Indian langur monkeys by Srivastava (1991), who suggests that this behavior, which is potentially dangerous to the mobbers, might function in "cultural transmission" of information. In her two observations, langurs approached the vicinity of a snake, screamed, and gave alarm calls. Unlike the data from the squirrel monkey report, Srivastava's data do not show that adults directed their behavior or calls specifically at immatures. The adults may simply have behaved as they normally would around snakes.

Many primates encounter snakes in their natural habitats, a fact that has led to interesting experimental work by Mineka and her colleagues on the transmission of "snake fear" among captive monkeys (e.g., Mineka et al. 1984; Cook et al. 1985; Cook and Mineka 1989). Naive juvenile rhesus monkeys, defined as juveniles with no initial fear of snakes, were the subjects of one set of experiments. Of six juveniles tested, five feared snakes after only eight minutes of watching models—their parents—behave fearfully in the presence of snakes. This result occurred even when the juveniles were tested in a context different from where the "observational learning" took place.

Other results obtained by this research team, in further experiments, show that models need not be relatives in order for the snake fear to be transmitted; and observers can discriminate between fear-relevant and fear-irrelevant stimuli. One experiment, for example, showed that naive rhesus monkeys acquired a fear of snakes simply by watching videotapes of two model monkeys reacting fearfully to toy snakes. The observer monkeys did not acquire fear, however, after watching videos of model monkeys showing exactly the same fear response to brightly colored artificial flowers. Such differential response points to some kind of prepared learning in which, because of past selection pressures in a species' ecological niche, some stimuli are more effective at eliciting responses than others. It is safe to assume that acquiring fear of snakes increased the reproductive success of the observers' ancestors more often than did acquiring fear of artificial flowers.

How exactly is snake fear transmitted from monkey to monkey? Rhesus

43

monkeys exhibit snake fear through what the researchers call "disturbance behaviors," including fear grimaces, threats, piloerection, and vocalization (no distinction was made between emotional and referential vocal communication). These behaviors clearly indicate, by means of highly visible and apparently "decodable" cues, an altered emotional state. In the wild, such cues might be effective enough to preclude the need for adults to physically protect or warn immatures, except in populations with heavy predation pressure, where such intervention might be selected for. In any case, these experiments point to a capacity for immatures to decode and utilize information acquired from adults—that is, to engage in information acquisition. What we do not know is whether adult rhesus monkeys direct their fear responses to immatures and thus donate predator-avoidance information to them.

Vocal-Auditory Referential Communication in Predator Avoidance

The predator-avoidance behavior of most primates includes vocal alarm calls, some of which are referential. All known examples of referential alarm vocalizations occur among monkeys, and the best-studied system of alarm calling among monkeys is that of the Amboseli vervets, researched by Cheney and Seyfarth. As Struhsaker (1967) first recognized, Amboseli vervets have multiple alarm calls, differentiated by predator. This makes them a likely population in which to search for information donation about predator avoidance; the relevant evidence has been conveniently summarized in Cheney and Seyfarth's *How Monkeys See the World* (1990), which also lists the scientific articles they have written on this topic.

Six acoustically different alarm calls have been identified in the Amboseli vervet population, one each for leopards, smaller carnivores, eagles, snakes, baboons, and unfamiliar humans. Using the playback technique, it was shown that in the absence of a real predator, vervets respond differently according to the specific call heard. When they hear an eagle call, for example, they look up into the sky or run into bushes; when they hear a leopard call, they run into trees. Although the alarm calls may contain emotion, they logically must also contain specific information about the type of predator seen when the call was originally uttered.

Evidence for information donation in this referential system appears to be mixed or to depend on one's interpretation. According to Cheney and Seyfarth (1990:225), "even in the most well-documented cases . . . active instruction by adults seems to be absent." Hauser, however, who also studied the Amboseli vervet population (Caro and Hauser 1992:161), cautiously implies the presence of teaching by concluding that "not only encouragement but also punishment may be important for the development of alarm calls." Hauser defines encouragement as the production of a same-type alarm call by a mature individual following, within five seconds, the production of an alarm call by the infant; punishment is a physically aggressive contact by one individual directed toward another who has just produced a contextually inappropriate call (Caro and Hauser 1992:161).

These slightly different interpretations may stem from the somewhat different observations produced by each study. For example, both research teams tried to discover whether adults alter their rate or type of alarm calling in ways that would suggest they are trying to guide antipredator behavior by immatures, facilitate predator recognition by immatures, or warn immatures specifically about impending danger. As Cheney and Seyfarth (1990:225) note, in any particular case of predator sighting, adults who do not initially give alarm calls often join in with the first caller and give "second alarms" of their own.

Sometimes adults do give these "reinforcers" to infants who have been the first to call correctly. Infants, however, make more mistakes than adults in producing alarm calls; that is, they give the call for the "right" predator in fewer cases. Despite this difference in error rate, adults are no more likely to give second alarms to infants who call correctly than to adults who do so. If second alarms serve to reinforce correct calling, they should be given to those who would benefit most from reinforcement and guidance—infants. Moreover, infants also made errors in response to alarm calls—for example, by looking up into the sky when they heard a snake alarm. According to Cheney and Seyfarth, mothers did not correct these errors, either.

Hauser presents additional data (Caro and Hauser 1992). In his study's sample of 68 alarm-calling bouts in which infants under one year of age were the first to call, adults encouraged infants in 34 cases. Of these, 26 cases occurred when the infant produced an appropriate call in the right context, but 8 occurred following the production of a call in an inappropriate context.

Looking at the consequences of encouragement is the next necessary step. Hauser analyzed consequences in three types of situations. First, when encouragement occurred after an infant gave an alarm call for the appropriate predator, the infant's next production of the same type of alarm call was heard in the appropriate context in 42 percent of cases and in inappropriate context in 15 percent (Hauser notes that data on subsequent calls were often unavailable). Second, when no encouragement occurred after an infant gave an alarm call inappropriately, the infant's next alarm calls were heard in appropriate contexts in 21 percent and in inappropriate contexts in 79 percent of cases. As Hauser suggests, one possible explanation of these findings is that second alarm calls by adults have a beneficial effect on the infant's knowledge of the association between call type and predator type. The third situation involved adult encouragement to infants' inappropriate alarms, which happened only once (see Caro and Hauser 1992:162). In four more cases, an inappropriate call was punished by the mother,

> who, after initially responding with flight, returned and physically attacked (e.g., bit or slapped) her offspring; in three out of four of these cases, the infant's subsequent and same-type alarm call was next heard in the appropriate context. Such aggressive interactions were never observed following inappropriate alarm calls by adults which, though infrequent, nonetheless occurred. As far as we know, therefore, this is the only demonstration of direct punishment under field conditions. Because most of the infants died before one year, however, it was not possible to compare their rate of vocal development with infants whose calls were not punished. (Caro and Hauser 1992:162)

Vervet immatures thus have information available to them, in vocal communication, about predators and predator-avoidance behavior. Some of this information may be donated to them by adults through encouragement or punishment, but it is apparent from both Hauser's study and Cheney and Seyfarth's that infants must acquire much of the information themselves. These data are particularly fascinating because they show that in a vervet population with high mortality due to predation, along with a sophisticated social system and referential communication, information donation about predation has apparently been selected for only weakly, if at all.

When infants do make errors in producing alarm calls, the mistakes are not random. Infant vervets tend to overgeneralize: they might give leopard calls for a wide variety of terrestrial mammals, including the harmless warthog. They do not, however, give eagle calls for warthogs. Gradually, infant calling does conform to adult patterns (Cheney and Seyfarth 1990; see Owings 1994 for a novel suggestion about infant errors). Presumably, the time it takes for an infant to acquire the information necessary for learning appropriate calls puts the infant at risk—a risk that may be decreased only minimally by information donation.

According to Seyfarth's (1986) review, acoustically distinct alarm calls are known to be given by a handful of other primates, and by many nonprimate mammals and birds. Whether these vocalizations constitute either referential communication or information donation or both remains to be seen in most cases (but for an interesting study of referential alarm calls in a nonprimate, see Slobodchikoff et al. 1991).

In both contexts considered in this chapter—social skills and predator avoidance—the relative contributions of adults and immatures to social information transfer seem similar. Donation of information from adults to immatures is apparently minimal in both cases. The capacity for such information donation seems to be present in some species—for example, in the direction or discouragement of certain social behaviors by immatures—but it is rarely expressed.

For firmer conclusions to be drawn, data are particularly needed that would (1) indicate that behavior increases in homogeneity over time when information is transferred from one animal to another (as required by a strict definition of social information transfer); (2) indicate whether or not modified behavior by adults constitutes teaching, that is, if infants truly acquire new skills or knowledge as a result of such modification; (3) allow information donation to be differentiated from information acquisition by focusing on whether or not behaviors or vocalizations are directed specifically at immatures; and (4) come from detailed field studies of apes, allowing better comparison between information transfer in apes and monkeys.

One striking pattern in the available data is consistent with a view of socialization as two way, with both infants and adults playing significant roles, rather than top down. Immature monkeys and apes have available to them many cues that may help them acquire information about social skills and predator avoidance. They are thus well equipped to deal with the challenge of surviving without much information donation. As the next chapter shows, the situation in foraging and tool use is quite similar—but the differences are exciting and may be significant for understanding the evolution of information donation in primates.

3

FORAGING AND TOOL USE IN
MONKEYS AND APES

Of all requirements for an animal's survival and reproduction, obtaining food is one of the most basic. Acquiring a species-typical diet and learning foraging skills are particularly important problems for primates because they must be solved so early in life. Once infant primates are weaned, although they still depend on their mothers in other ways, they must supply 100 percent of their own nutrition; they get no food from adults. Only in humans (among primates) does postweaning survival become a collective responsibility. As Lancaster (n.d.; Lancaster and Lancaster 1983, 1987) has pointed out, humans do what other primates do not: provision juveniles. Humans provide food to their offspring for many years beyond weaning, and as a result, human juveniles die at a lower rate than do ape or monkey juveniles. Human foragers and apes are similar in such life-history parameters as birth spacing, fertility rate, and reproductive lifespan. The feeding of human juveniles likely accounts for their increased survivorship and, in turn, for long-term population expansion in humans (Lancaster n.d.).

Learning what and how to eat is especially challenging for immatures in primate populations that have very selective diets. Omnivores, by definition, eat a wide variety of foods, but they are often choosy about which food parts to eat. A vast amount of information must be acquired by immature omnivorous primates.

Three major problems must be solved by all foraging animals and may be especially complex for omnivores (see also Cant and Temerin 1984). First, food is not always easily visible. Not all primates can locate food as readily as, for example, the herbivorous mountain gorilla (*Gorilla gorilla beringei*). Gorillas travel, rest, groom, and play right in the middle of their food supply and can usually reach out and find food whenever they get hungry. For many species, the search for food is more complicated. Food items may be hidden altogether, perhaps underground (Andersen 1987), or the visible portion may be inedible, such as the hard shells encasing some fruits and nuts. Obtaining hidden foods like these qualifies as *extractive foraging* (Parker and Gibson 1977, 1979), a behavior that will play an important role in the ideas presented in this volume.

Second, gorillas and other primates must do more than simply find food and eat it: they must also combine items appropriately to obtain a balance of nutrients and avoid toxins. Choosing foods in the condition that offers maximal nutrition may be accomplished by selecting ripe fruit rather than unripe, or mature leaves instead of young ones (Milton 1979). Toxins can cause problems ranging from outright poisoning to incomplete digestion (Glander 1982) and thus present a real challenge for immatures; trial-and-error experimentation is not the safest way to learn about poisons (see Whitehead 1986).

Third, in order to locate and eat food, foragers must travel through their habitat in such a way as to maximize benefits (food) while minimizing risks. They must, for example, conserve energy during travel, avoid predators, and minimize contact with competitors when resources are limited. When moving about, foragers probably take into consideration the distance between resource patches and the distribution of risks within those patches (e.g., Kummer 1982; Sigg 1986).

For infants, yet another problem arises—one that derives from their early dependence on the mother for nutrition. Until they are fully weaned, infants must also adjust to their mothers' preferred activity patterns. The transition from suckling to nutritional independence is not sudden. In her study of Amboseli baboons, J. Altmann (1980) showed that weaning is a process whereby the mother conditions her infant to what she considers the proper time for suckling and contact. As the infant ages, its mother restructures the timing of suckling bouts to fit her own schedule. When the infant reaches about four months of age, its mother begins to discourage it from suckling or contact at the very times that were previously acceptable to her. The infant is now discouraged from suckling while the mother forages, apparently because suckling interferes with her ability to feed. The infant must instead make contact with its mother during rest periods. Similar conditioning occurs in other primate species, including rhesus macaques (Johnson 1986).

A Foraging Case Study: Baboons of Kenya

A good illustration of problem solving in foraging comes from savanna baboons, omnivorous cercopithecine monkeys that live in multimale, multifemale groups. The social structure of savanna baboons is matrilineal, which means that female-female kin relationships are typically friendly and supportive; males usually emigrate from their natal groups at puberty, and thus tend to be unrelated within any one group. Savanna baboons have been well studied by primatologists and are the subjects of my own research. For these reasons, offering an extended case study of baboon foraging makes a good first step in considering the relative roles of immatures and adults in primate foraging.

By the time I went to Kenya to study baboons, a great deal was known about foraging (e.g., Altmann and Altmann 1970; S. Altmann, personal communication; D. Post 1978, 1982) and about infants (e.g., J. Altmann 1980) in the Amboseli population. S. Altmann had identified baboons as eclectic omnivores, noting that despite their broad diet they are selective in two ways. Adult baboons choose food items carefully from among a wide array of potential sources, apparently in order to escape nutritional deficits and secondary compounds. In addition, they extensively manipulate various foods to separate the edible and nutritious parts from parts low in nutrients or high in toxins.

Post (1978, 1982) had similarly found that almost half of adult feeding time was devoted to parts of only two species, the fever tree (*Acacia xanthophloea*) and a grass, *Sporobolus kentrophyllus*. According to Post, baboons' favorite food is corms, the underground storage organs of grasses such as *S. kentrophyllus*. The year-round availability of corms helps baboons survive the dry season, when many plants die or lose nutrient value.

Infant baboons at Amboseli were known to depend heavily on their mothers for suckling and transportation during the first six months of life, with some dependence lasting throughout the first year. After their first birthday, most infants could probably survive their mother's death (J. Altmann 1980:142). Early attempts at independent feeding by infants were not guided by adults: "The only way that group members provide food for a baboon infant, other than its mother via lactation, is through tolerance of infants at a food source, the result of which is that infants obtain scraps of foods that they themselves could not obtain by their own effort" (J. Altmann 1980:171).

How infant baboons acquire the diverse but selective diet of an eclectic omnivore had not been investigated in any depth. This general question, as well as the specific ones I mentioned in chapter 1, formed the basis of my study in Amboseli. The precise questions of interest to me now, however, did not crystallize until I returned from the field. I set out to study how infants acquire foraging skills, which is different in subtle and important ways from directly investigating social information transfer. For that reason, my measurements of some baboon behaviors are not directly applicable to the evaluation of social information transfer. Research designed to focus specifically on that subject will produce firmer conclusions than the ones drawn from this case study.

For 13 months at Amboseli, I observed the food-related behaviors of 19 infants between 2 and 32 weeks of age, in two baboon groups (table 1). The data presented here are based on 1,013 hours of observation dating from November 1985 to November 1986. I used three types of sampling techniques: focal animal, scan, and ad libitum (J. Altmann 1974; see King 1989 for details). Focal

TABLE 1
Data on infant baboons at Amboseli National Park, Kenya

Infant (n=19)	Sex	Group Affiliation	Birthdate	Point	Focal	P+F
Tuzo	M	Hook's	24 May 85	8	6	14
Modem	M	Hook's	21 Aug 85	12	7	19
Dumu	M	Alto's	21 Aug 85	10	7	17
Odin	M	Alto's	1 Sep 85	12	6	18
Alfa	F	Alto's	1 Sep 85	11	7	18
Viva	F	Alto's	20 Sep 85	16	9	25
Pambo	F	Hook's	19 Oct 85	21	11	32
Limau	F	Hook's	31 Oct 85	21	13	34
Chyulu	F	Alto's	8 Nov 85	21	9	30
Nick	M	Hook's	14 Jan 86	32	20	52
Kelly	F	Hook's	3 Feb 86	38	18	56
Wallis	M	Hook's	16 Feb 86	38	22	60
Sudi	F	Alto's	20 Mar 86	46	31	77
Luna	F	Hook's	22 Jul 86	35	20	55
Bitir	F	Alto's	7 Aug 86	20	14	34
Janja	F	Alto's	18 Aug 86	19	8	27
Franklin	M	Alto's	28 Aug 86	16	6	22
Paka	F	Alto's	9 Sep 86	14	4	18
Kitok	M	Hook's	25 Sep 86	18	5	23
Total	9M	9 Hook's				
	10F	10 Alto's		408	223	631

Point = number of 15-minute point samples.
Focal = number of 15-minute focal samples.
P + F = total samples excluding ad libitum.

animal and scan are formal sampling techniques that force the observer to focus systematically on certain behaviors in one or several subjects at a time. They are designed to avoid bias (for example, an emphasis on the most obvious behaviors or most active animals) and to yield data that can be analyzed statistically. Ad libitum is a more casual type of sampling in which the observer may look for specific behaviors but in which the selection of subjects need not be random or restricted. Ad libitum sampling produces qualitative data.

In this section I present both quantitative data and qualitative data in the form of anecdotes. Currently there is renewed debate about the role of anecdotes in scientific research (see Whiten and Byrne 1988). I agree with primatologists who claim that anecdotes are important complements to hard data (e.g., Smuts 1985; Goodall 1986; Whiten and Byrne 1988). It is true, as Bernstein (1988) has written, that the plural of "anecdote" is not "data"; it is impossible to evaluate either the importance or representativeness of single observations of behavior. But although anecdotes cannot replace quantitative data, there are studies—including those of social information transfer and social learning—in which anecdotes take on special importance and should be published. Rare occurrences that have no statistical significance may instead have great biological significance. Single cases of social interaction can be important in the social transmission of behavior, and the experiences and actions of one animal can affect others in significant ways (Strum and Mitchell 1987; Hauser 1988; Stanford et al., n.d.). Primatologists who report anecdotes will eventually create a rich fund of observations on these topics.

In my study of infant foraging, anecdotes are important for another reason: they show that despite devoting a small part of the day to actual feeding, the infant baboon constantly experiences opportunities for information transfer about foraging from adults. On the average, baboon infants in my sample spent 29 percent of their time suckling and 11 percent of their time feeding independently. (Recall that I sampled only infants 32 weeks of age and younger; if data had been taken on older infants, the percentage of time spent feeding independently would certainly have been larger.) One-tenth of the day devoted to independent feeding is not much. Weanlings, the youngest juveniles, feed for 42.1 percent of their total time (S. Altmann, personal communication) and adults for 46.4 percent (Post 1978). Food-related interactions or experiences of only a few seconds are difficult to represent quantitatively, but they attest to the potential for significant daily amounts of information transfer.

In addition, infants often did not ingest what they sampled. For reasons related to the definition of feeding adopted by previous Amboseli researchers, manipulation or touching of food was scored as feeding in all the Amboseli feeding studies cited here, including mine (see King 1989). My impression is that infants contacted foods without ingesting them at a higher rate than did adults.

My data support two conclusions about infant foraging at Amboseli. First, virtually no information donation occurs. Second, infants behave in a way consistent with the use of social interactions to increase the potential for acquiring information about foraging from adults. That is, infants seem to set up opportunities for information acquisition. This phenomenon is best illustrated by activities known as cofeeding, tolerated scrounging, and muzzle-muzzle behavior.

Cofeeding may be defined broadly, as Nicholson (1982:64) does in her study of savanna baboons, as "mother and infant feeding simultaneously within

one meter of each other." Despite this precise wording, Nicholson acknowledges that cofeeding may also involve infants and conspecifics other than the
mother. Indeed, other adults or older animals of any age may be important
feeding partners for the infant baboon.

When two baboons feed simultaneously, regardless of the food items
chosen, I term it *feeding synchrony*. I reserve the term *cofeeding* for the situation in which a pair of baboons not only feeds at the same time but chooses
items from the same food type. "Food type" is a subjective classification meant
to reflect broad similarities in available foods. In recording feeding behavior, I
noted the food part eaten using a list of "core foods" adapted from the work
of S. Altmann (personal communication). Altmann found that Amboseli weanlings spent 93 percent of their feeding time on just 52 core foods, although
there were 277 different foods in their diet altogether. Recording the core
foods eaten, along with any foods that fall outside the species-typical diet,
should provide a clear and reliable indicator of infant diet. Core foods as I have
grouped them into food types are listed in table 2.

Cofeeding, then, is a subtype of feeding synchrony. Results related to both
behaviors are based on 321 scan samples of 15 minutes each on the 14 oldest
baboon infants in my overall sample. Feeding synchrony and cofeeding with
the mother occupied 58 percent and 37 percent, respectively, of total infant
feeding time. That the infant opted more than half the time to feed when its
mother did is not surprising, because at this early age the infant and its mother
are in close proximity (J. Altmann 1980; King 1989). Infants co-fed with other
baboons as well, including their nearest neighbor, defined as the baboon (excluding the mother) nearest to the infant within 5 meters. Feeding synchrony
and cofeeding with the nearest neighbor took up 39 percent and 27 percent,
respectively, of total infant feeding time.

The typically small distances between foraging baboons, along with the
patchy nature of some baboon foods, may partly explain the fairly large amount
of cofeeding between infants and older group members. Another finding, however, is not readily predictable from knowledge of baboon social relationships
or ecology. Cofeeding with the mother and sometimes with the nearest neighbor was not independent of the food type on which the infant fed. As table 3
indicates, infants co-fed both with the mother and the nearest neighbor at a
higher rate on corms, and at a lower rate on leaves and stolons, than on other
food types. An intermediate amount of cofeeding occurred with fruit, seeds,
and tree gums. It appears that infants cofeed with older baboons more often
when those older animals feed on hard-to-process foods. Corms are almost
surely harder for baboon infants to process than are fruits, for example, which
in turn seem harder to process than leaves or stolons.

Although intriguing, this correlation between cofeeding and the processing difficulty of foods is only tentative. Precise measurements of the processing

TABLE 2
Baboon "core foods" at Amboseli National Park, grouped into six food types

Food Type and Number	Description	Scientific Name
Corms		
1		*Sporobolus kentrophyllus*
2		*Sporobolus cordofanus*
3		*Cyperus obtusiflorus*
4	Other or unknown	
Leaves/stolons		
5	Green leaves	*S. cordofanus*
6	Green leaves or stolon	*Cynodon nlemfluensis*
7	Green leaves	*Suaeda monoica*
8	Green leaves	*Lycium europaeum*
9	Green leaves	*Salvadora persica*
10	Green leaves or stolon, other or unknown grass	
Fruit		
11	Ripe berries	*Azima tetracantha*
12	Green berries or berries of unknown ripeness	*A. tetracantha*
13	Ripe berries	*S. persica*
14	Green berries or berries of unknown ripeness	*S. persica*
15	Fruit	*Commicarpus plumbagineus*
16	Fruit	*Trianthema ceratosepala*
17	Fruit	*Tribulus terrestris*
18	Fruit	*Withania somnifera*
19	Fruit	*Capparis tomentosa*
20	Ripe fruit	*Solanum coagulans*
21	Other ripe fruit	
22	Other green fruit	
Seeds		
23	Fever tree seeds from green pods	
24	Fever tree seeds from brown pods	
25	Fever tree seeds loose on ground	
26	Tortilis tree seeds from green pods	
27	Tortilis tree seeds from brown pods	

Continued on next page

TABLE 2—Continued

Food Type and Number	Description	Scientific Name
Seeds		
28	Tortilis tree seeds loose on ground	
29	Fever or tortilis tree seeds in dung	
Gum		
30	Fever tree gum	
Other		
31	Fever tree blossoms	
32	Tortilis tree blossoms on tree	
33	Tortilis tree blossoms on ground	
34	Blossoms	*L. europaeum*
35	Other blossom	
36	Blade base	*Sporobolus consimilis*
37	Green blade base, other or unknown grass	
38	Green seedhead	
39	Wood	*S. persica*
40	Other wood	
41	Other item from wood	
42	Dung beetle larvae	
43	Invertebrate	
44	Vertebrate	
45	Mushroom	
46	Lily	
47	Other from dung	
48	Other on ground or from plant	
49	Water, ground source	
50	Unknown	

Note: "Pods" refers to pods either intact on trees or fallen to the ground.

TABLE 3
Cofeeding of infant baboons with mother and nearest neighbor at Amboseli National Park

			Food Type		
	Corms	Leaves/Stolons	Fruit	Seeds	Gum
With Mother					
n	10	13	14	8	11
%	76.1	22.8	51.5	55.5	56.8
SD	22.3	17.5	36.7	34.1	27.8
With Nearest Neighbor					
n	10	13	14	8	11
%	50.1	13.7	46.4	41.3	33.9
SD	28.2	20.2	35.5	34.6	31.8

n = number of infants out of 14 exhibiting that behavior.

% = percentage of the total number of infant feeding bouts on the specified food type; percentages within a food type may equal more than 100 because infants sometimes co-fed with both mother and nearest neighbor.

SD = standard deviation.

difficulty of various primate foods are lacking (but see Kinzey and Norconk 1990). Alternative explanations may exist. Perhaps there is a correlation between the distribution of certain food types and the distribution of feeding baboons: if corms (but not other food types) are clumped so that baboons feed on them synchronously, with no other foods available nearby, then my finding might after all be explained by ecology. Infants might cofeed on corms only because no other foods are available nearby and they want to stay near adults. This is a doubtful explanation for selective infant cofeeding, however. Other baboon foods appear to be clumped; it is unlikely that corms are distributed uniquely. Furthermore, independent feeding takes up a small part of infants' time budget. Even if infants are surrounded by corm-feeding baboons, they need not cofeed or even feed at all. They could investigate the environment, play with peers, or carry out some other activity.

The apparent correlation between cofeeding and food type carries implications for information acquisition. Infant baboons seem to create opportunities to acquire information from adults in just those areas where information would help them the most. Corms are nutrient rich and available year round, and thus very much worth obtaining—but because they are located underground, they may be impossible for the youngest infants to get. Until about six months of age, infants lack the strength or dexterity to pull corms up from the soil (Altmann and Altmann 1970). Cofeeding with adults on corms thus makes sense for infants. When adults dig and eat corms, infant cofeeders can observe and practice selecting and processing certain corms over others. This apparently selective behavior on the part of infants is reminiscent of Pereira's (1988) finding discussed in chapter 2: that juvenile baboon males and females at Amboseli associate selectively with adults in just the ways that probably best prepare them for adulthood.

Many simple experiments could be conducted to test whether selective cofeeding occurs in primates. Captive adults and infants of various species, for example, could be given an array of items to eat—some easy, some difficult, and some impossible for the infant to process. Their behavior might then yield data to help answer questions such as, Do infants direct different food-related behaviors, or food-related behaviors at different rates, toward adults when the adults eat hard-to-process foods? If the items that are most difficult to process are also the most nutritious or most preferred, does infant food-related behavior change? Do adults ever guide infants' food choices or demonstrate processing techniques to infants, and if so, do these behaviors increase as the processing difficulty of available foods increases?

A behavior related to cofeeding is tolerated scrounging, defined as one baboon's allowing another to take food scraps from or from around its body. Tolerated scrounging is a form of exploitation of labor (Altmann and Altmann 1970:154); baboons of both sexes and all ages regularly exploit the labor of others while foraging (Post 1978; J. Altmann 1980; Stein 1984; Byrne and Whiten 1985; Shopland 1987). For example, when an adult male baboon kills a gazelle, he is surrounded by other baboons who try to scrounge scraps of meat; tolerated scrounging may be the only low-cost way for others to get access to a prized food. Adults sometimes supplant others from a foraging site and then consume the partly processed food items left there. Rarely are infants able to supplant adults, but by taking scraps they do obtain food that has been partially processed. Tolerated scrounging can be considered a form of information acquisition because immatures use it to obtain both food and information about foraging.

When near adult males, Amboseli infant baboons scrounge scraps of corms more than any other food (Stein 1984:230). Qualitative data from my study suggest that corms are the preferred food for infants to scrounge, whether from their mother or their nearest neighbor. Selective tolerated scrounging must be confirmed with more data. Such confirmation would be exciting: this behavior seems adaptive for the infant for reasons similar to those of selective cofeeding, but with one difference. Tolerated scrounging allows young infants access not only to information about a hard-to-process food but also to the food itself. Unlike cofeeding, tolerated scrounging directly affects an infant's nutritional, as well as its informational, intake.

Tolerated scrounging is frequently mentioned in reviews of primate foraging (e.g., Feistner and McGrew 1989) but is rarely explored empirically. Anecdotal evidence, however, provides some insight into this behavior. First, tolerated scrounging allows infants to obtain food items that otherwise would be inaccessible. From my field notes, 15 May 1986: *Infant female Limau, age 196 days, watches attentively as her mother digs up a white, potato-sized tuber from about 6 or 8 inches beneath the ground. Limau and an unrelated male juvenile eat scraps of the tuber.* Tolerated scrounging can also be used in conjunction with attempts at independent feeding. Feeding on corms, another below-ground food, illustrates this mix of behaviors by infants. (Note that *S. kentrophyllus,* the preferred corm of adults, seems more difficult for baboons to pull up than other corms.) From 10 August 1986: *Infant female Kelly, age 188 days, sits less than 1 meter from an adult male and eats scraps of the corms* (S. kentrophyllus) *that he eats. Occasionally she succeeds in digging up such corms on her own using her teeth, but clearly has difficulty in doing so.* And from 28 March 1986: *Infant female Viva, age 189 days, eats scraps of corm* (S. kentrophyllus) *taken from her mother and other adults. From time to time, Viva tries to dig up her own corms, but does not succeed. She resumes scrounging. Other young infants in the group dig other corms that appear easier to uproot.*

The scraps available to infants for scrounging do not always correspond to the food parts eaten by adults. Sometimes scraps are available because adults discard nonpreferred parts. An infant baboon may rest against its mother's belly or chest as she feeds from the green leafy plant *Trianthema ceratosepala,* the fruit (or ovary) of which is a core food for adults. The scraps that fall onto the infant's head and coat usually consist of the ovary wall or green leaves, not the ovary itself, which the mother eats. Parts rejected by adults are thus often the ones with which infants gain experience. By strict definition, this type of tolerated scrounging is not social information transfer, because it cannot lead to increased homogeneity of behavior between infant and adult. But could this kind of tolerated scrounging affect the foraging skills acquired by infants? Do infants first scrounge a "wrong" plant part and then select it to eat when foraging independently? If so, then the potential strategy that Galef terms "matching-to-scraps," in which an immature learns about its group's diet by tasting scraps of adults' food and then matching the taste during independent feeding, would backfire.

In fact, young infants do sometimes sample "wrong" parts when feeding on their own, but the reason may lie in their lack of strength or dexterity rather than in interaction with adults. Infants do not ignore food plants until they have all the skills necessary to eat the "correct" part. Rather, they gain experience with those plant parts they can handle, and later eat the same parts that adults eat. In the meantime, the "wrong" part may or may not be sampled or eaten.

From my field notes of 20 March 1986: *Infant male Wallis, age 32 days, mouths leaves of the* Trianthema *plant as his mother eats the ovaries. Scraps fall onto Wallis's body; they are either pieces of the ovary wall or of green leaves.* From 9 May 1986: *Wallis, now age 82 days, attempts to pluck off the ovary from the* Trianthema *plant but instead succeeds only in getting a green leaf. He discards the leaf and again tries pulling at an ovary, but the ovary does not come off. He abandons the plant without eating any leaves.* Soon after this observation, Wallis succeeded in eating some ovaries and continued to do so regularly.

The relationship between tolerated scrounging and information acquisition is not fully understood. Both quantitative data on and careful description of tolerated scrounging are needed for a variety of primates. Does tolerated scrounging correlate with certain diets or with eating hard-to-process foods? If some infants are tolerated as scroungers by adults more often than others, do they benefit by getting better nutrition? How often do infants scrounge the "wrong" parts of foods? As with cofeeding, these and similar questions could be investigated both in captivity and in the wild.

A third food-related behavior observed in Amboseli infants is muzzle-muzzle behavior, sometimes called muzzle sniffing, which is defined as one baboon's placing its muzzle within an inch of another baboon's muzzle. The initiator of the behavior can inspect, using vision and smell, the recipient's nose and mouth, although the sensory nature of the inspection itself is too subtle to be measured reliably in the field. Many primatologists (e.g., Altmann and Altmann 1970:154; Kummer 1971:126; Goodall 1973:154; Nicholson 1982:54; Takasaki 1983:273; Smuts 1985:267; Hiraiwa-Hasegawa 1990a:267) have observed and commented upon muzzle-muzzle behavior, but I am unaware of any attempts to systematically record or classify it.

I observed 435 instances of muzzle-muzzle behavior during my study, not only when formally sampling infants but also during ad libitum observation of all age-sex classes. It is thus possible that my observations are biased (see J. Altmann 1974) rather than systematic. Nevertheless, three aspects of the observed pattern of muzzle-muzzle behavior suggest that immature baboons can use muzzle-muzzles to get information about diet from adults (table 4).

First, immatures initiate more muzzle-muzzles than would be expected if initiations occurred at frequencies proportionate to the number of immatures and adults in each group. In one of the two groups I observed, immatures initi-

TABLE 4
Observed frequencies of initiators and recipients of muzzle-muzzles by baboons at Amboseli National Park

	Average Number	*Initiator*	*Recipient*
Hook's Group			
Adult male	7	0	15
Adult female	16	55	150
Immature male	16	62	18
Immature female	15	101	35
Total	54	218	218
Alto's Group			
Adult male	13	6	10
Adult female	19	47	166
Immature male	16	73	14
Immature female	18	91	27
Total	66	217	217

Average Number = average number of animals in that age-sex class over the course of the study.

ated 74.8 percent of muzzle-muzzles, although they made up only 57.4 percent of the group on average over my study period. In the other group, immatures initiated 75.6 percent of muzzle-muzzles, despite making up only 51.5 percent of the group on average.

Second, adults in both groups received disproportionately more muzzle-muzzles (75.7 percent and 81.1 percent in the two groups) than would be expected based on their contribution to group size (42.6 percent and 48.5 percent of group size, respectively). Third, muzzle-muzzles occurred more often than expected in the context of feeding. Each muzzle-muzzle was classified according to the recipient's activity—feeding or chewing, not feeding or chewing, or activity unknown. Most muzzle-muzzles were received during feeding or chewing: 78 percent of all cases in one group, and 81 percent of all cases in the other. Post's (1978) data show that feeding takes less than 50 percent of the adult time budget. Thus, muzzle-muzzles do not occur in proportion to the time spent on various behaviors in the overall time budget. Although these three measures are imperfect ones for assessing information transfer, they do indicate that muzzle-muzzles are more likely to be related to foraging than, for instance, to some type of greeting behavior. An immature may use them to acquire information about foraging by sensory inspection of the adult's muzzle and thus of the adult's food choice.

My call for more precise data collection relating to social information transfer is by now familiar. Better data that are amenable to statistical analysis are needed for muzzle-muzzle behavior just as much as for cofeeding and tolerated scrounging. One relevant research question might be, Do adult baboons receive muzzle-muzzles from infants at a higher rate when eating unusual or rarely obtained foods than when eating common ones? I observed some instances of this kind of behavior, although infrequently. From my field notes of 20 November 1985: *An adult female raids a van filled with tourists who are photographing the baboons. She grabs a green vegetable from somewhere in the van, sits in the road, and begins to eat it. Immediately she is surrounded by older infants and young juveniles who initiate muzzle-muzzles with her.* From 10 September 1986: *A juvenile male eats scraps of meat (Thompson's gazelle) that he obtained from an adult. He receives muzzle-muzzles from two unrelated infant females as he eats.*

It would also be interesting to know how often the initiator of a muzzle-muzzle follows up by immediately eating the same foods that the recipient of the behavior had been eating. On 8 May 1986 I observed: *An infant male muzzle-muzzles an unrelated adult female as she eats a large grasshopper, then he eats scraps of the insect.* From 27 August 1986: *An infant male sits near an unrelated infant female who feeds on an unidentified, berry-sized item. The male reaches for her hands, then muzzle-muzzles her. The food item falls out of her mouth, and the male puts it into his own mouth.* Only with much detailed information of this type, taken over the long term, could we assess whether muzzle-muzzle behavior is a good example of information acquisition in foraging.

I have put forth a view of the baboon infant as an active participant in information acquisition. More data from the testing of specific hypotheses would help distinguish this perspective from an alternative one—that immatures' acquisition of foraging skills is facilitated primarily by certain features of baboon social organization (S. Altmann, personal communication). Within a baboon group, social bonds between infants and their mothers and other matrilineal kin are extremely important. Infants associate closely with female relatives and are allowed to observe much of their behavior. Furthermore, baboons preferentially direct altruistic behavior toward matrilineal kin. According to the alternative view, an infant's behavior in acquiring various species-specific skills is largely a byproduct of the features of baboon social organization that promote association with and toleration of the infant. Many of the patterns suggested by my data are, indeed, likely to be facilitated by baboon social organization. In my view, however, the data also support the suggestion that infants actively participate in, and sometimes initiate, food-related behaviors that may result in information transfer.

Insight into information donation by adult to immature baboons comes, in my data, only from anecdotes; no incidents of information donation took place that can be analyzed statistically. Anecdotal evidence largely shows an absence of concern on the part of adults for infant foraging behavior. Consider an observation from 12 February 1986: *Infant female Limau, age 104 days, chews dried palm fronds and wood from the trunk of a palm tree* (Phoenix reclinata). *These items are not eaten by adults. Three minutes after ingestion, Limau vomits. Throughout this sequence, Limau's mother sits within arm's reach of Limau, but facing away from her. She shows no reaction or interest during this sequence. Another infant female briefly chews palm fronds after Limau does so, but this infant does not vomit.*

This observation raises more questions than it answers. Was Limau's mother unaware of her selecting and eating foods from the palm tree—items that fall outside the population-typical diet? Why didn't she pay more attention to Limau's behavior at the palm tree? Was she capable of connecting Limau's vomiting with her daughter's behavior of three minutes earlier? If so, did she fail to punish her daughter's actions because, after all, vomiting is punishment enough? Perhaps for Limau this event constituted one-trial learning, which can effectively alter diet choice in primates. Physiological punishment may be more effective than any intervention on the part of the mother.

Evidence for intervention by adult baboons in the feeding behavior of immatures is weak at best. I saw only nine instances of what might be classified as food-related intervention by adults. All but two of these can be explained as an adult's trying to discourage an infant from interfering in its own feeding. For example, from 8 October 1986: *Infant male Sudi, age 202 days, feeds at the same bush* (Azima tetracantha) *as does his mother. Twice, as Sudi reaches out for ripe fruits, his mother hurriedly plucks and eats those particular fruits.* Had Sudi's mother picked and then discarded the fruits, it could be argued that she was guiding her infant's food choice. Because she ate the fruits instead, her behavior seems more consistent with the interpretation that she interfered with her infant's foraging in order to get ripe fruit for herself. I saw no evidence of directed maternal action in this case or the six others like it. The absence of directed action (rather than features of the mother's probable intent) is the key, and it indicates that information donation was not present.

Two cases of adult intervention in infant foraging did not involve adults taking food from infants or defending their own food source. From my field notes of 24 April 1986: *Infant male Wallis, age 67 days, picks up one stalk of consimilis grass* (Sporobolus consimilis) *and mouths the blade base. His mother manually removes the stalk from his mouth.* From 26 August 1986:

Infant female Luna, age 35 days, handles and mouths the stem or stolon of a grass that her mother is eating. A short time later, she picks up the same kind of stem in her mouth. At this time, her mother is being groomed a short distance away by Luna's aunt. The aunt glances up from grooming and manually removes the stem from Luna's mouth.

What sense can be made of these two instances? Neither involves infant experimentation with foods outside the diet of the baboon group, a likely context for information donation. In neither case did the infant avoid the grass in subsequent foraging bouts. The key element is that adults did guide infant food choice, and the two instances therefore meet the definition of information donation. It cannot be ruled out, however, that the adults' actions might have been attempts to stop something aversive to them, as was the case in the other seven examples. During the observation of Wallis just described, he rode ventrally on his mother as he mouthed the grass stalk, and the stalk brushed against her coat. Perhaps this irritated her and led her to remove it from his mouth.

These two cases of apparent information donation in foraging are very few when considered against the total hours of observation. I saw no cases of infants being punished by adults for food-related behavior, as illustrated by the example of Limau and the palm tree. Nor did I observe any instances of adults actively sharing food with infants. The baboon infant is very much on its own in solving foraging problems after weaning. Future research on baboons and other primates might be able to track the long-term consequences of infants' differential abilities to take responsibility for information acquisition about foraging.

How does the situation as outlined in this case study compare to that for other primates? Can any conclusions be generalized from infant baboons to other primates? And how often do adults in other populations donate information about foraging, or food itself, to immatures?

Infant Foraging in Other Primates

The literature on primate foraging suggests two generalizations about the relative roles of adults and infants in social information transfer. First, most primate infants are responsible for getting both food and information about foraging on their own, as are Amboseli baboons. Infants rarely receive donations of food or information from adults, although the exceptions are enlightening. Second, infants cope with this challenge in a variety of ways.

Exceptions to the first conclusion provide a good place to start. True food sharing, as opposed to tolerated scrounging, does occur in some primates. When food is voluntarily transferred from adult to infant, information about diet and food choice is also transferred. The most elaborate system for voluntary food donation is found among the New World callitrichids (Feistner and McGrew 1989). These monkeys—the marmosets and tamarins—are small bodied, usually monogamous, and territorial. Unlike most primates, callitrichids routinely raise twins; and males and older siblings contribute significantly to infant care. This family-based reproductive system provides a likely context for true food sharing, which has been observed in several species.

In wild buffy-headed marmosets (*Callithrix flaviceps*), infants sometimes initiate the transfer of food items from other group members. The food is given up willingly, however, and older monkeys sometimes give food to infants without prompting (Ferrari 1987). These marmosets transfer both food and information to infants and thus demonstrate information donation. A similar phenomenon occurs in captive tamarins (*Leontopithecus rosalia*) when adults give a call inviting others to share their food (Brown and Mack 1978). Food sharing has been seen in other callitrichids (Feistner and McGrew 1989) and can be expected to occur in other monogamous, family-living primates as well.

Further evidence of food sharing comes from the great apes. Orangutan mothers (*Pongo pygmaeus*) put juice and chewed foods onto their hands, which they then place near the mouths of infants six months or younger (Horr 1977:307). Bonobo mothers occasionally strip skin from sugarcane, break off a piece, and hold it in their mouths without chewing until their juveniles take the food (Kano 1992:165). A few cases of voluntary food donation in chimpanzees are known, at least one involving an infant: a mother donated figs to her infant with no apparent prompting (Ghiglieri 1984:74; see Goodall 1990:212 for an example of apparently compassionate food sharing, although not to an immature).

The transfer of food items among chimpanzees, however, has been described most often as tolerated scrounging or as the solicitation of food by infants. Hiraiwa-Hasegawa's (1990a) report from Mahale, Tanzania, offers some precise data on infant solicitation, defined to include the infant's extending a hand to mother's food or mother's mouth, attempting to take a food item directly from mother's hand, or initiating a behavior equivalent to muzzle-muzzle. During their first year, Mahale infant chimpanzees solicited food almost once every three minutes during maternal feeding. Their solicitation rate varied according to food type. During the infant's first six years, it was higher for "difficult" than for "easy" foods; difficult foods were defined as those that the infant was unable to procure or process independently.

Hiraiwa-Hasegawa found no evidence to suggest a similar alteration of maternal behavior when difficult foods were eaten: mothers' willingness to tolerate scrounging or share food did not vary along that dimension. Two earlier studies in the wild showed that chimpanzee mothers at Gombe do transfer

Figure 1. Rhesus macaque females surround a five-day-old infant. The three adults are, from left, the infant's grandmother, mother, and aunt. Photo taken at Cayo Santiago, Puerto Rico, by Courtney A. Snyder. Courtesy Courtney A. Snyder.

Figure 2. A two-year-old male chimpanzee places his lips at his mother's mouth in a begging gesture as she eats leaves and an egg. His mother shared some of the food after this picture was taken. At right is the infant's five-year-old sister. Photo taken at the Gombe Stream National Park, Tanzania, by Janette Wallis. Courtesy Janette Wallis.

Figure 3. An adult female baboon, Dottie, and her son, Dumu, an older infant, cofeed on corms. Photo taken at Amboseli National Park, Kenya, by B. J. King.

Figure 4. An adult female baboon, Willie, feeds on corms,
closely followed by her young son, Wallis. Photo taken at
Amboseli National Park, Kenya, by B. J. King.

hard-to-process foods to their infants more readily than other foods (McGrew 1975; Silk 1978). In all these reports for Gombe and Mahale chimpanzees, as with mine for Amboseli baboons, processing difficulty affects the food-related behaviors of immatures, if not also of their mothers, in some way.

Voluntary food donation qualifies as information donation and probably as teaching because immatures' food choices are directly guided by adult behavior that is modified from the norm. What other types of information donation occur in primate foraging? Nishida (1986) suggests that primate adults use discouragement and encouragement of certain behaviors as ways to teach immatures. Discouragement and encouragement may, indeed, meet the criteria for teaching employed in this book.

Adult chimpanzees occasionally guide infants' food choices by discouragement. The evidence is anecdotal but important because interventions occurred when infants experimented with foods outside the population-typical diet and because adults apparently received no immediate benefit from their own actions. Goodall (1973:154) gives three examples in which adult chimps interrupted infant feeding to remove and discard an unusual food item from the infant's mouth or hands. In each case the intervention was carried out by an older female relative (twice the mother, once the sister). Similar instances have been recorded at Mahale (Nishida et al. 1983:177; Hiraiwa-Hasegawa 1990b). In one, the mothers of two infants snatched away a piece of papaya and some leaves of "an unusual plant" from their offsprings' mouths and discarded them. Neither food is eaten by adults. Among mountain gorillas, a few similar incidents have been observed (Fossey 1979; Watts 1985).

One problem with assessing information donation in foraging is that we lack basic knowledge about how group members exchange or share information during foraging. Learning more about this general topic would provide primatologists with clues to how adults might be donating information to immatures in subtle ways. A promising approach is to study cooperative hunting as a subtype of foraging in which social information transfer is likely to occur in particularly sophisticated ways. Data are not available concerning adult-to-infant information transfer during cooperative hunting, but despite this gap, analysis of cooperative hunting is relevant because it should generate hypotheses about the nature of adult-to-adult information exchange during foraging, and in turn about information donation from adults to immatures in a number of foraging contexts.

Many primates hunt invertebrate and vertebrate prey (Butynski 1982; Cheney and Wrangham 1986). The typical procedure is for an individual forager to search for and/or capture prey on its own. Some form of coordination among hunting individuals, however, has been studied extensively at three major primate sites—Gilgil, Kenya, for savanna baboons (Strum 1981); and

Gombe, Tanzania (e.g., Teleki 1973, 1981; Busse 1978; Goodall 1986), and Tai National Park, Ivory Coast (Boesch and Boesch 1989), for chimpanzees. Because these studies have employed varying definitions, it is necessary to operationalize a few terms.

Strum (1981) observed two kinds of systematic prey capture in Gilgil baboons: simple and complex hunting. Compared to simple hunting, complex hunting involved more than one baboon predator and lengthier pursuits of prey in terms of both time and distance. Not all complex hunts involved some kind of coordination among the predators, but some did, including those in which five baboons moved synchronously over 1,600 meters to locate a prey animal, and then spent more than two hours following, searching for, and chasing the prey (1981:260). The key behavior here is synchrony of movement. As described by Strum, this behavior and others, such as sequential chases of the same prey by several males, clearly imply close monitoring and probably information exchange of some sort, unlike a situation in which several individuals converge on the prey accidentally or out of fortuitously similar goals. Strum refers explicitly to coordination (1981:262) and communication of intent among hunters (1981:281) and discusses how males monitor each other's actions, but she does not discuss specific mechanisms of information transfer.

In describing coordination among chimpanzee hunters, Goodall also uses the term *cooperation,* which she defines as the action of two or more chimpanzees directed simultaneously toward the same goal, making it more probable that the goal will be attained (1986:285). Goodall provides some intriguing examples of cooperation in hunting, including one in which five chimpanzees surrounded a male colobus monkey in a tall tree. The chimpanzees deployed themselves in various positions so as to cut off the monkey's escape routes. For fifteen minutes, the monkey tried to dodge the apes, but the chimpanzees repeatedly acted in coordination to block its escape and eventually succeeded in capturing it.

As with the vast majority of such descriptions of chimpanzee behavior, there are no clues in this anecdote about the type of communication used among the hunters. In one case of Gombe male chimpanzees hunting bushpigs, however, a communicative signal was described: "Figan, after gazing intently into a thicket where a sow and piglets had run, looked back at Jomeo and gave the characteristic branch shake that is normally used to summon females during consortships. Jomeo at once hurried over, both males entered the thicket, and a piglet was captured" (Goodall 1986:287).

The observation and description of such a signal is significant because it strengthens the case for true cooperation as opposed to accidental convergence of movement or other goal-directed behaviors. For Gilgil baboons and Gombe chimpanzees, many questions arise: When do males monitor each other's behaviors and adjust their own as a result? When do they signal each other about their own intentions or desires, as Figan apparently did with Jomeo? Are male hunting partners ever recruited actively? Strum (1981:275) notes that among the Gilgil baboons, all incidents ending with cooperation began with what appeared to be individual efforts, an interpretation counter to the notion of active recruitment in baboons.

More attention has been focused on describing hunts according to type of prey (Goodall 1986) and on assessing the outcome of hunts—for example, whether or not the size of a hunting party and its success in capture are related (Busse 1978; Teleki 1981)—than on describing the precise nature of the communication and coordination among hunters. It is hard to understand why. The visual, gestural, and auditory signals given by potential hunting partners might be subtle, but presumably they would be noticeable to experienced fieldworkers. Does their absence in descriptive accounts mean that they are, indeed, absent, or that primatologists are rarely attuned to them during the fast-moving events of the hunt?

Recognizing the various levels of complexity that might be involved in cooperative hunting, Boesch and Boesch (1989:550) provide definitions of four types of hunting organization among chimpanzees at Tai: (1) similarity, in which hunters concentrate similar actions on the same prey, but without any spatial or temporal relationship between the hunters; (2) synchrony, in which each hunter concentrates similar actions on the same prey and tries to relate them in time to the others' actions; (3) coordination, in which hunters relate not only in time but also in space to each other's actions toward the same prey; and (4) collaboration, in which hunters perform different, complementary actions toward the same prey. At sites where these four types of hunting can be distinguished, it should be possible to test the hypothesis that complexity of information transfer (measured as visual, gestural, and auditory signaling as opposed to only monitoring of others' behavior) increases as one moves up the proposed hierarchy of hunting complexity.

At Tai National Park, according to Boesch and Boesch (1989), chimpanzees hunted with partners in 92 percent of cases and used the collaborative technique of complementary actions in 68 percent of the cases for which hunting technique could be determined. My inference is that for complementary actions to be achieved, exchange of information among hunters *must* occur—yet on the basis of available data, the picture remains unclear. The Boesches attempted to determine the point at which "a hunt is decided and according to what signal" (1989:554). In half the hunts observed during a two-year period, intent to hunt was clearly noted during prey searches but before any prey were seen or heard. (Searches involved the chimpanzees' being silent, remaining close together during movement, and stopping regularly to look up into trees.)

While these data may indicate that hunts are often initiated in the absence of some signal from prey, they do not address the question of signals among hunters. Boesch and Boesch (1989:558) do note that larger hunting groups have greater success than smaller ones. They even say that the chimpanzees are "apparently aware" of this fact, an inference they justify by noting that

> the first lone hunter behaves so as to attract more hunters rather than trying to catch the prey on his own. He will follow the prey slowly, making them produce alarm calls. Sometimes his behavior may even look *deceitful,* in that he gives "hunting barks," although he is never in the situation that normally elicits such a call, i.e., rapidly pursuing or about to capture a prey. If no chimpanzees join the hunt, he will normally stop.

Thus we see how one male hunter may attract others, but we still lack insight into the question of information transfer during the hunt itself. If Tai chimpanzees rely on collaborative hunting more than Gombe chimps, as the Boesches suggest (but see Stanford et al., n.d.), do they also rely on more complex information transfer? Is there a relationship between phylogeny and cooperative hunting—for example, do baboon hunters coordinate themselves in space and time less frequently or efficiently than do chimpanzees? Are the Boesches' four categories applicable to baboons? Unfortunately, trying to answer some of these questions is complicated by the Gilgil baboons' having ceased hunting in the complex manner described; no other baboons have been observed to hunt in a cooperative way (Strum 1981).

Other questions target immatures and ask if the pattern in which infants must acquire their own information about foraging applies to meat eating, meat capture, and eventual participation in hunting. Immatures apparently do not take part in coordinated hunting at the three sites described, but they become increasingly involved in meat eating and capture as they grow up (see particularly Strum 1981:276–77). One generality noted for both baboons and chimpanzees is that association with preferred adult males affects an immature's participation in features of meat eating such as carcass investigation and tolerated scrounging. These behaviors are apparently the first steps in a sequence that might eventually lead to hunting, or are at least necessary prerequisites to hunting (Strum 1981; Boesch and Boesch 1989). Perhaps immatures must acquire their own information about skills related to meat and hunting, with information exchange coming into play only during cooperative hunts among adults, when it might serve to increase each hunter's chance of success.

Cooperative hunting is only one example of a behavior that involves information transfer from adults to adults rather than across generations. Other examples might include hamadryas baboons' "voting" on the direction of group travel (Kummer 1968:128–30), and sophisticated cooperation in coalitions and alliances among primates in general (Harcourt 1992). The study of communication among primate adults in these situations might help primatologists understand how foragers of all ages transfer information to each other about foraging techniques and about food items themselves.

Another logical place to look for information donation in foraging is in primates' food-related vocalizations. In the previous chapter, referential communication was discussed in terms of social behavior and predator avoidance, and a major problem was noted: because referential calls, or responses to them, are rarely known unquestionably to be directed toward immatures, they cannot always qualify as information donation. The same problem exists for primate foraging. Moreover, fewer studies of referential communication during foraging have been carried out, and even fewer included playback experiments. An example that illustrates these problems is Dittus's (1984) report on Sri Lankan toque macaques (*Macaca sinica*), which has received much attention from primatologists and other ethologists.

According to Dittus, toque monkeys give food calls when they discover large amounts of high-quality food. Dittus suggests that the calls are referential because of their association with two features of the food—abundance and quality. This interpretation is open to criticism, however:

> Although most of the food calls were given upon the discovery of ripening fruit trees and other high-quality food, approximately 3 percent of the calls were given to changes in season, either to the first rains at the end of the dry season or to the first sunshine at the end of the monsoon. These calls would be described more parsimoniously as *euphoria calls*. It is not clear that the reference is limited to food, and the restriction to location of high-quality foods as well as to positive seasonal changes suggests a motivational rather than a symbolic function for these calls. (Snowdon 1990:230)

Most primates, of course, have food-associated calls of some type, and many of the calls probably encode both referential and motivational information. The challenge for scientists is to cleanly separate and then measure the two aspects. Hauser and Marler (1993a) have shown that the Cayo Santiago rhesus macaques, for example, produce five acoustically distinct calls in the context of food. Two of these call types, the coo and the grunt, are used also in nonfood contexts; the grunt, but not the coo, varies acoustically from one context to another. The coo call is thus unlikely to be part of a referential system in which specific information is communicated to other individuals (Hauser and Marler 1993a), but this still leaves four referential, food-associated calls.

Grunts are associated primarily with the monkeys' consumption of commercial chow on Cayo Santiago, whereas the other three types of calls (warbles, harmonic arches, and chirps) are given by animals who possess a rare and valued food item. In the course of a day, the call rate changes with the apparent motivational state of the monkeys (as measured by food consumption and thus relative hunger versus satiation) but the call type does not. The researchers therefore conclude that although the precise functions of calls remain unknown (are they labels for food? requests for others to eat?), Cayo Santiago rhesus monkeys use call structure to encode information about food, and call rate to encode information about motivational state. (See Hauser and Marler 1993a for information about variation in call production according to sex and social status, and Hauser and Marler 1993b for contexts of call production versus suppression.) Food-associated calls of the type identified by Hauser and Marler are likely to be widespread in primates and to aid in information acquisition and donation regarding food.

Considering together the available data on food sharing, discouragement of food choice, and vocal communication, I conclude that in all but a few cases infants must acquire food and information about foraging on their own, with little active guidance from adults. Voluntary food sharing constitutes the type of information donation most often observed in primates, with discouragement of food choice second; known instances of both come from just a few species. Voluntary food sharing constitutes directed action toward an immature. It may also *select for* increased levels of information donation, if food sharing itself correlates with difficult-to-process foods; this idea is pursued later in the book.

As a footnote to this discussion of information donation, it is worth mentioning that adult primates not only fail to help immatures in foraging, but they also sometimes seize foods from immatures. Examples of this behavior are reported by Feistner and McGrew (1989). In one case, captive stumptail macaque (*Macaca arctoides*) and rhesus macaque infants, but not adults, had access to preferred foods through a tiny hole in their cage. Infants ate some items and filled up their cheek pouches with more. When they returned to the adults, "their mothers forcibly removed these items from the infants, even from within their cheek-pouches, albeit with vigorous vocal and physical resistance from the infants. The latter soon learned not to return to their mothers until the food-items had been consumed" (Feistner and McGrew 1989:24). In the wild, bonnet macaque (*Macaca radiata*) mothers take food directly out of their infants' hands and mouths (Simonds 1965).

If most primate immatures must get their own information about foraging, how do they do it? The importance of solicitation and tolerated scrounging to chimpanzee infants has already been discussed. What other behaviors of immature primates might function in information acquisition about foraging? Is active participation in information transfer, as opposed to observation and imitation alone, widespread among primate infants? As Galef (1991) has remarked, primatologists have a long history of claiming that infants learn about foraging through observation and imitation (e.g., Kawamura 1959; Jay 1963; Goodall 1973, 1986). The assumption underlying this viewpoint is made clear in Cambefort's (1981:244) report on the cultural transmission of feeding habits in baboons and vervet monkeys: "When primates are born, they are unaware of their later diet, the only food known being milk. The later diet will have to be learnt during childhood, at first by observing the mother and later by watching other group members."

Risks involved in the invoking of social learning were discussed in chapter 1; many of the same problems impede the reliable documentation of imitation, especially in field research. The role of imitation in the ontogeny of tool use will be discussed later. For now, suffice it to say that two limitations hamper a thorough examination of foraging in immature primates: the difficulty of pinpointing how immatures acquire information about foraging from adults (a problem at least until more primatologists adopt social information transfer as their focus), and the scarcity of careful studies of the subject. Four recent studies, all characterized by research on wild primates in relatively undisturbed habitats, show how these problems may be remedied.

Whitehead (1986) studied mother-infant pairs of wild mantled howling monkeys (*Alouatta palliata*) in Costa Rica and tested for differences between social and individual learning in foraging. He used specific criteria to evaluate learning by social means: the infant must look at the model animal while feeding; the infant's feeding must be restricted to periods when the model feeds; the model should intervene when an infant eats a nonpreferred food part; infants that fail to attend to the model should eat some unpalatable plant parts; and an infant must not eat items outside the model's or the social group's diet. Whitehead observed only two mother-infant dyads in this way, presumably because of the intensive nature of the research combined with the challenge of looking for fine details of behavior in arboreal animals. Even so, Whitehead's conclusions are meaningful. Infant howling monkeys learned which leaves to include in their diet by social means. Mothers more often ate leaves before infants did, for example, than the other way around. Fruits, in contrast, were chosen by infants independently of social learning. Infants sampled fruits and fruitlike objects that adults did not eat.

Whitehead relates his results to the higher levels of toxins found in leaves than in fruits. For infants, the conservative approach is to minimize danger by learning about leaves from adults. Notice how this result varies from that of my cofeeding study among Amboseli baboon infants; at Amboseli, leaves are apparently not treated as risky. For howling monkeys, a casual approach to eating fruits is appropriate because fruit eating carries fewer risks. Whitehead's study acccords with the view that infants are able to acquire information from adults in just those situations where it would be most helpful. Howling monkey infants, however, may play a less active role in information transfer than do Amboseli baboon infants. They appear to rely on observation and imitation to the exclusion of other techniques for getting information. It is also worth noting that adult howling monkeys were not observed to taste novel plant parts when accompanied by infants, but did so at other times. Although true information donation may be absent, adults do seem to have adjusted their behavior when infants were present; that is, by acting cautiously concerning food experimentation.

Different but equally compelling results were obtained from Boinski and Fragaszy's (1989) study of Costa Rican squirrel monkeys, the same study population in which adults donate information to immatures about predators (see chapter 2). The evidence suggests that infants rarely monitor experienced foragers, including their own mothers. Infants were unlikely to be close to another monkey that was foraging. Weaning was accomplished, nonetheless, over a period of only six weeks. By four and a half months of age, most infants foraged in the same way older animals did. As the authors state, this is a rapid developmental sequence for a primate. Boinski and Fragaszy conclude that many skills needed by squirrel monkeys can be acquired without long-term practice. Infants seem not to be active participants in acquiring information from older foragers.

The disparity between this finding for squirrel monkeys and Whitehead's for mantled howling monkeys raises a series of questions. Why should these two South American species differ so greatly in the degree to which infants use interaction with adults to acquire information about foraging skills? Is one situation or the other more typical of the primate pattern in foraging? Do certain aspects of diet or intelligence correlate with these systems? Milton (1981, 1988), in her comparison of howler monkeys (*Alouatta palliata*) and spider monkeys (*Ateles geoffroyi*), discusses some of these issues.

Milton begins her comparison of howler and spider monkeys, which are sympatric in her study area of Panama, by noting their similarities. Both are arboreal, are about the same size, and eat mostly plants (but lack physiological specializations for doing so). Spider monkeys eat much more fruit than howlers do. Differences in foraging behavior are profound, the most critical of them involving what Milton calls "the information unit." For howler monkeys, the social group acts as the information unit. The group is cohesive, even during foraging. If an infant stays with the group, it acquires population-typical diet and foraging skills gradually, without heavy reliance on long-term bonds with older animals. Indeed, the period of maternal dependence in howlers is brief. The infant travels and feeds independently by six months, although it continues to suckle at that age.

For spider monkeys, the individual is the information unit. Acquiring information about foraging is more complicated for the infant than merely staying with the group and doing what group members do. The spider monkey group does not feed as a unit; foraging is done in small subgroups and sometimes alone. For infants, a two-year period of intense association with the mother is critical to acquiring information. According to Milton, imitation of actual food choice is important, but, unlike the case in howlers, direct experimentation is important too. Milton relates spider monkeys' willingness to experiment to the relative lack of toxins in fruits as compared to leaves, a distinction similar to the one Whitehead made for howling monkeys.

Why should the foraging systems of howler and spider monkeys function so differently and yet each so efficiently? Milton suggests an answer that arises from another difference between fruits and leaves. Unlike leaves, fruits tend to occur in scattered patches, and their locations and times of ripening are unpredictable. Primates that eat large amounts of fruit are therefore under different, harsher selection pressures than are more folivorous, or leaf-eating, species. Evidence suggests that patchy distribution of food sources may correlate with increased mental development and intelligence in an array of mammalian species (see chapter 5). The important point here is that in two species of primates that are relatively closely related, infants face vastly different foraging problems and may differ in cognitive complexity as a result. Although, as usual, more data are needed, both social information acquisition and donation seem more common in spider monkeys, whose infants have more information about foraging to gain than do howler monkey infants (but see Milton 1993). Milton's conclusions about howler monkeys thus accord well with Whitehead's in their suggestion that observation and imitation, and not other forms of social information transfer, are the chief means of acquiring information about diet.

So far in this section only monkeys have been considered. Little precise research has been done on the ontogeny of feeding in great apes; the best study to date is Watts's (1985) on the mountain gorillas of Rwanda. Although he does not use the same terms, Watts presents anecdotal information about cofeeding and tolerated scrounging by immature gorillas. The two infant gorillas he observed were very likely to eat the same food as that being eaten by their mothers, or foods the mothers had been eating earlier in the same feeding bout. Infants' first experiences with food items involved scraps from maternal feeding. Watts mentions that "nose-to-mouth" behavior, presumably the equivalent of muzzle-muzzle behavior, did not occur in gorillas.

Like the howling monkey, the folivorous mountain gorilla shows little evidence of information donation. Infants do seem to acquire information in ways that go beyond imitation or observation. When precise data are collected on the more frugivorous, or fruit-eating, western lowland gorilla (see Tutin et al. 1992), comparison of mountain and lowland gorillas along the lines of Milton's comparison of two New World monkeys will be possible.

A fifth study, although not done under natural feeding conditions, is noteworthy for its innovative focus and its conclusions about the food-related behavior of infants. Bard (1990) videotaped five immature orangutans during their twice-daily provisioning in Indonesian Borneo. Behavioral categories, scored during data collection from videotape, classified attempts by immatures to get food and the responses of mothers to those attempts. Bard found that even young infants manipulated their mothers to obtain food items from them. Over time, the intentional *behavior* of young infants developed into the more sophisticated intentional *communication*—the ability to obtain food through indirect manipulation of a social agent, the mother. Early manipulative sequences included pulling on parts of the mother's body to get food (intentional behavior); later, infants used begging gestures, but did not actually manipulate the mother's body, to motivate the mother to give food (intentional communication). Although mothers sometimes shared food voluntarily, they more often tolerated food-related behavior from the infant or ignored and rejected the infant. Apparently the burden is on the infant to initiate some kind of food-related action from the mother. Bard notes that this type of manipulative behavior is equivalent cognitively to tool use, which is observed routinely in captive but very rarely in wild orangutans.

In sum, the responses of infant primates to the need for acquiring information about foraging vary according to factors such as species, diet, and social organization. Many infant primates are active participants in information transfer, more so than would be expected from their widespread reputation as passive observers and imitators. Information donation in foraging, however, occurs in only a few species, so far as we know. At this point no generalizations can be made about the exact role of the infant in information acquisition for foraging skills.

In the overwhelming majority of cases, primates forage without the use of technology. When primates use tools to obtain food, immatures must acquire special skills in addition to the ones already discussed, and so tool-aided foraging provides a good context for studying information donation.

Tool Use in Primate Foraging

Tool use is more common in primates than in other mammals but has been observed, nevertheless, in few primate species (Candland 1987), especially in the wild. Tool-using behavior is best known for one great ape, the chimpanzee, and one New World monkey, the cebus (but see Beck 1980 and Candland 1987 for other examples). Primates use tools more often for food acquisition than for defense, attack, or grooming (Candland 1987). In the remainder of this chapter, I will consider participation by immature and adult primates in tool use that relates to foraging.

Beck (1980:10) defines tool use as "the external employment of an un-attached environmental object to alter more efficiently the form, position, or condition of another object, another organism, or the user itself when the user holds or carries the tool during or just prior to use and is responsible for the proper and effective orientation of the tool." Note that Beck excludes from the definition certain types of object manipulation. Suppose two apes, sitting side by side in a tree, try to open some hard-shelled fruit. The first ape picks up a stone and pounds it against the fruit, while the second ape smashes the fruit itself against the tree trunk. According to Beck's definition, only the first ape is a tool user because the second ape did not hold or carry an unattached object as the tool. Although these two examples of fruit-opening techniques cannot be used to distinguish between the problem-solving abilities of the two apes, Beck is right to favor a conservative approach when it comes to identifying tool use.

A Case Study of Tool Use: Chimpanzees of Ivory Coast

The most famous primates in the world are the chimpanzees at Gombe Stream, Tanzania, studied for the last three decades by Jane Goodall and her colleagues. It was Goodall who first discovered tool use and manufacture among chimpanzees. Typical contexts for tool use at Gombe and at nearby Mahale are insect collection, drinking, and self-grooming. These behaviors, observed and analyzed in detail, are complex (e.g., Goodall 1973, 1986; Teleki 1974; McGrew 1979, 1992; Nishida and Uehara 1983). The use of sticks or vines to "fish" termites out of mounds, for example, requires six separate steps (Teleki 1974; Tomasello 1990:276): a chimpanzee must locate a passageway leading to the termite mound's interior and scratch a hole for access; select an appropriate tool that is firm yet pliable; modify the tool to make it free of leaves and twigs; place the tool into the mound's passageway at the proper depth; wiggle the tool to cause the termites to bite it; and extract the tool without shaking the termites free. That immature chimpanzees do not become proficient at termite fishing until at least five years of age attests to the difficulty of this sequence.

At Gombe and Mahale, all tools used by chimpanzees have been made of organic materials such as sticks, grass, and leaves. Until recently, organic tools were considered typical for the species (although limited evidence for stone tool use by chimpanzees was known for West Africa; see Hannah and McGrew 1987). When rainforest chimpanzees are studied, however, a different picture of tool use emerges. Since 1979, Boesch and Boesch (1981, 1983, 1984, 1990; Boesch 1991, 1993) have observed a community of about 80 chimpanzees at Tai, Ivory Coast (the same chimpanzees profiled earlier in the section on cooperative hunting). Their published reports are the source for all data presented in this case study. Among their most startling discoveries: Tai chimps use stone tools in sophisticated ways, and some mothers actively guide their infants' tool behavior.

Tai chimps use organic tools to collect insects and in other ways similar to those of Gombe and Mahale chimps. They also use both organic and stone tools as hammers to open nuts (primarily *Panda oleosa* and *Coula edulis*) that are tough to crack. A typical nut-cracking sequence unfolds as follows: A chimpanzee gathers nuts and carries them to a tree root. She positions a nut in a depression in the root, which acts as an anvil, and pounds the nut with a hammer. This pounding maneuver often requires precise control. Inside the *Panda* shell, for example, are three or four almonds arranged in a circle; opening the nut without destroying the almonds is tricky. Once the nuts are opened and eaten, the chimp usually resumes her search for nuts, perhaps changing anvils as she goes.

The use of female pronouns in this description is appropriate. Female chimps at Tai are more efficient at nut cracking than males and are almost exclusively responsible for using the more difficult of a range of nut-cracking techniques, such as opening *Panda* nuts (McGrew 1979 reports a similar sex difference at Gombe). Boesch and Boesch see evidence in both sexes for complex skills such as memory for tool location and selection of tools appropriate to the job at hand.

Young chimpanzees have much information to acquire before they master nut cracking, which is considered by Boesch (1993:174) to be "the most demanding manipulatory technique yet known to be performed by wild chimpanzees." It is nonetheless astonishing, given the long period of immaturity in apes, that nut cracking is mastered only in adulthood. Between infancy and the time when nut cracking is perfected, mothers donate nuts and information directly to their offspring. Such behavior, which in some instances fits the definition of teaching, constitutes the most sophisticated case of information donation yet known to primatology (but see Galef 1992).

Nuts, shared by the mother, provide a critical source of nutrition during the first eight years of a Tai chimpanzee's life. Daily during the nut season, mothers get 3,800 calories from nuts and give up as many as 1,000 calories in nuts to infants aged three to five years. Mothers donate information as directly as they do food. They place nuts or tools in ways that encourage nut cracking by infants. Mothers also improve their infants' nut-cracking efficiency by providing the nuts or tools most likely to result in successful nut cracking. One mother watched her infant "struggle unsuccessfully" with the hammer tool (Boesch 1991:532). With her offspring sitting in front of her, the mother then slowly and deliberately rotated the tool into the most effective position for pounding the nut, and cracked ten nuts. The infant adopted and maintained the position of the hammer as demonstrated by her mother. Mothers thus modify their behaviors at a likely cost to themselves and with likely benefits for their infants, which accords well with the definition of teaching.

Why should nut cracking with tools and active guidance of nut-cracking techniques occur among some chimpanzees but not other primates? One hypothesis—that some difference in the cognitive abilities of apes and monkeys accounts for monkeys' seeming inability to perform these behaviors—fails to explain why Tai chimps crack nuts and guide their offspring's attempts at doing so, whereas chimps at Gombe and Mahale do not. All the raw materials needed for nut cracking are present at Gombe, and the motor patterns used in nut-cracking techniques have been seen occasionally in Gombe chimpanzees (Goodall 1986:563). The apparently greater degree of food sharing at Tai may be an important clue to these cross-populational differences. A link between the systems of food sharing and nut cracking at Tai has been explored by Boesch (1993) and is discussed in some depth in chapter 5.

So far, data collected at Tai inform us mainly about the adult role in behaviors related to nut cracking. The adult role is fascinating because it involves previously unknown levels of information donation to immatures—but it gives clues to only half the story. How does the chimpanzee infant contribute to information transfer about nut cracking and other aspects of foraging? At Gombe, infants interact a great deal with their mothers during adult tool-using behavior. With so much for infants to learn at Tai, especially during nut season, I predict that infants as well as adults participate actively in information transfer. The role of the infant is a promising topic for future research at Tai.

Patterns in Foraging-Related Tool Use

This section analyzes evidence for the ontogeny of tool use (meaning "tool use as related to foraging") in primates, specifically in chimpanzees and cebus monkeys. Unfortunately, few data are available from wild primates (but see Beck 1980 for an invaluable chapter devoted to this topic in wild and captive animals). Tantalizing data from captive primates are beginning to fill gaps in our understanding, but in many cases are preliminary. Nevertheless, it seems clear that little active donation of information from adults aids immatures in acquiring tool-use skills.

McGrew (personal communication) reports that chimpanzee mothers at Gombe tolerate their offspring's frequent interruptions of their termite fishing. For example, an infant may attempt to collect termites missed by its mother, sometimes directly off her current or abandoned tool. Maternal response to this interference varies; sometimes the mother switches to another tool and allows the infant to take her current one. (See McGrew 1977:284

for a contrast in infant behavior during ant-dipping.) Goodall (1986:561), in a broad assessment of the situation at Gombe, suggests that youngsters learn community-specific patterns of tool use "through a mixture of social facilitation, observation, imitation, and practice—with a good deal of trial and error thrown in."

Young chimpanzees may be forced to yield to adults at tool-use sites even if the young were there first. Goodall (1986:539) notes one particularly relevant instance of this, although the age of the offspring, Pom, at the time of the observation is not given. During one dry season, when it was difficult to fish for termites,

> Passion [the mother] noticed that Pom had found a productive site. At once she moved across and displaced her daughter, who then sat and watched as Passion tried, with little success, to work the passage. After twenty minutes Passion gave up and left the heap. Pom immediately returned and once more fished very successfully. After eight minutes Passion, who had been feeding nearby but out of sight, reappeared with a grass stem in her mouth. Once again she displaced Pom. Once again she failed where Pom had succeeded. After fifteen minutes she moved off, leaving the site to Pom. This time the young female worked continuously for twenty minutes, catching some termites (although fewer than at first). Passion reappeared, once more with a tool in her mouth, and made a final attempt to replicate her daughter's success. Failing again, she left for good. Pom persisted for another thirteen minutes, after which she went off after the rest of the family.

I quote this passage at length because it echoes a situation that arises in foraging behavior without tools, in which adults may actually hinder their offspring's foraging. A similar anecdote (Goodall 1990:166) involves a mother who not only displaced her daughter from a termite-fishing site but also seized her daughter's tool for her own use. Goodall does not indicate the frequency of such occurrences or whether adults encourage or discourage various attempts at tool-using by young infants.

Beck (1982) has noted a trend toward "chimpocentrism" within ethology. It is often assumed rather than tested that chimps are more intelligent than other animals and rely on observational and other forms of social learning to a greater extent. Results from captive studies challenge Goodall's suggestion that social learning and imitation are important in the ontogeny of chimpanzee tool use. Laboratory-reared chimpanzees with no opportunity to observe conspecifics poke sticks into holes in ways similar to those used by their wild counterparts during termite fishing (Gould 1986). Perhaps infants at Gombe could learn to fish for termites without observing older chimps. On the other hand, Gombe chimps grow up to use tools differently from chimps at Tai, which suggests that interaction with and observation of others do affect infant behavior even if they aren't strictly necessary for the development of that behavior (compare Tomasello 1990 and Boesch 1993 for differing views about cultural transmission in chimpanzees).

A chimpocentric view is ameliorated also by attention to the behavior of cebus monkeys. Wild cebus monkeys use tools in more diverse contexts than any other type of monkey (Parker and Gibson 1977), although they do so in fewer contexts than those found in chimpanzees. In captivity, cebus monkeys use sticks to obtain out-of-reach food and use pounding objects to crack open nuts or molluscs; similar pounding behavior has been observed sporadically in the wild (Visalberghi 1987:169). Little is known about tool use itself in wild cebus monkeys, much less about its ontogeny (Visalberghi 1990). Some sophisticated types of object manipulation seen in the field are not definable as tool use in Beck's sense. In Colombia, for example, black-capped capuchins (*Cebus apella*) strike cumare fruits against trees to open them (Izawa and Mizuno 1977). Two different techniques are used, depending on the ripeness of the fruit. Immatures sometimes fail to open fruits because they acquire these techniques only gradually.

Might imitation, as opposed to observation, play a role in the ontogeny of tool use? Although other behaviors might be transmitted by imitation as well, I have not explored that possibility for two reasons hinted at in chapter 1. First, my intention is not to differentiate among types of social learning, and second, imitation, just as much as other forms of social learning, is notoriously difficult to distinguish under field conditions (but see Hauser 1988). Recent observations and experiments, however, have focused questions of imitative ability on primate tool use and have generated new interest among primatologists in imitation.

Many forms of imitation can be identified (see Galef 1988), but only one, true imitation, generates new behaviors through observation alone rather than through direct experience (Galef 1988; Russon and Galdikas 1993). In true imitation, "an imitator attends to a model's actions then undertakes to replicate them in a purposeful, goal-directed way; observation of the modeled actions is sufficient instigation for the replication" (Russon and Galdikas 1993:147). As Russon and Galdikas point out, true imitation can occur only once in any attempt to reproduce a given behavior, because subsequent attempts must reflect some kind of experience on the part of the imitator.

Although the criteria used to study imitation vary, the best attempts in both captive and field settings incorporate aspects of the preceding definition. Visalberghi and Fragaszy (1990:251), working with captive cebus monkeys, considered that behavior is imitated when an individual performs a behavior similar to that of a model's, where "similarity" must be defined ahead of time, where observation of the model is necessary for the behavior's production, and where the behavior is novel in a dimension in which novelty is usually absent. Regarding novelty, once again an a priori decision is needed, and what is meant by "a dimension in which novelty is usually absent" will vary across species. Cebus monkeys, for example, routinely pound various objects on various substrates. Choosing a new object to pound would not fulfill the novelty criterion (Visalberghi and Fragaszy 1990).

In their study of ex-captive orangutans, Russon and Galdikas (1993) identified spontaneous imitation by looking for similarity to a known model plus contingeny on the model. That is, for an incident to count as imitation, the reproducer must have little chance of spontaneously performing the behavior without some kind of modeling. Precise criteria were used in this study to measure imitation and to justify the claim that the reproducer would not have performed the behavior without a model (see Russon and Galdikas 1993 for details).

Issues similar to those discussed in chapter 1 for social learning, then, must be confronted when assessing a role for imitation in primate social information transfer. Galef (1988) doubts that imitation will ever be documented reliably, because controlling for each and every alternative is so difficult. Methodological rigor in captivity and the field may provide a more hopeful perspective; the question then becomes whether imitation plays a role in information acquisition concerning tool use in foraging. Monkeys and apes enjoy a reputation as "clever copiers" (Fragaszy and Visalberghi 1990:162). Because of this reputation, the results from recent captive research may be surprising: "Monkeys do not seem to be capable under common circumstances of learning tool use by imitation. The data for apes are scantier, but suggest similar, although less severe, limitations" (Visalberghi and Fragaszy 1990:269).

Visalberghi (1990) found that among cebus monkeys, for example, when a tool-use problem was presented to a social group, only some monkeys learned to use the tool. This result by itself does not rule out imitation, because individuals could vary in their imitative capability. But two other observations, added to the first, argue against a significant role for imitation: much interindividual difference and high levels of trial-and-error behavior were seen in the solving of tasks.

In chimpanzees, true imitation may not differ qualitatively from what is known for cebus monkeys (Tomasello 1990; Visalberghi and Fragaszy 1990). Most studies claiming to show the existence of imitation in chimpanzees used no proper controls. In fact, only one study (Tomasello et al. 1987) has directly compared the performances of chimps who observed a model's tool use with those of chimps who did not. Imitation did not occur in that study, although only those chimps with access to a model acquired the tool use.

A different view is provided by the work of Russon and Galdikas (1993), mentioned earlier, which does not focus on tool use in foraging but which has implications for the study of imitation in foraging-related tool use. A central goal of their research with ex-captive orangutans at Tanjung Puting, Indonesian Borneo, was to recognize and understand the inconsistency between the rich imitation identified observationally and the impoverished imitation commonly found in experiments. Both humans and other primates, they point out, are highly selective in choosing to model only certain actions of only certain models. Their data back up this contention. They observed 354 imitative "reproductions" by 26 orangutans. Of these, 54 were considered complex, involving more than just one simple action; at their most complex, the reproductions required multiple steps in sequence. Most of the 54 complex reproductions involved tool use (see Russon and Galdikas 1993 for detailed qualitative observations).

A significant finding relates not only to what the orangutans imitated but whom they chose as models:

> Our imitators selected their own models and those they chose were overwhelmingly individuals or groups with whom each imitator had well-established, stable and positive affective relations (parental, friend); experimenters have tended to preselect models, with no apparent attention to models' relationships with subjects.

Russon and Galdikas's research (see also Boesch 1993:178) thus highlights an important methodological problem in captive studies—the experimenters' preselection of models. Does this method weaken the conclusions about imitation derived from those studies? More research of the kind Russon and Galdikas did, and propose, is needed before any judgment can be reached.

If imitation turns out to be relatively unimportant or difficult for primate infants, how *do* those infants acquire tool-use skills? In the captive experiment reported for chimpanzees (Tomasello et al. 1987), in which the performance of chimpanzees who observed a model's tool use was compared with that of chimpanzees who did not, the model's behavior apparently served to direct observers' attention to the objects involved in, and the consequences of, tool using. In acquiring tool behavior, observation of the model was coupled with the chimpanzees' "natural capacity for tool-use cognition" (Tomasello 1990:287). Information donation is not indicated, because the observer's attention was apparently attracted to the model by the model's doing something interesting, not by any behavior directed by the model to the observer.

Other factors that constitute neither information donation nor information acquisition, as defined here, have been implicated in the learning of tool-use behavior as well. Trial and error seems to be an important factor for both cebus monkeys (Visalberghi 1990) and chimpanzees (Goodall 1986). Some data reflect an association between tool-use competence and previous experience in playing with or manipulating objects (see McGrew 1977; Beck 1980; Parker and Poti 1990). As immatures grow, innate actions may first be performed, then eventually combined, and finally applied toward specific goals (Parker and Poti 1990).

Visalberghi and Fragaszy (1990:267) conclude that "coaction of a skilled model and a learner" is the most effective way for primates to learn novel motor skills. Coaction qualifies as information donation because it includes the model's motor guidance of the observer and the model's allowing the observer "to participate intimately in its actions" (Visalberghi and Fragaszy 1990:267). I agree that this behavior, which is expected to be restricted to mother-infant pairs, would be extremely effective, but I know of few cases in which it has been documented. The behavior of chimpanzee mothers at Tai and Gombe in guiding their offspring's tool behavior certainly qualifies as coaction, as does one example from cebus monkeys at a testing apparatus that involves the use of a stick to probe for syrup (Westergaard and Fragaszy 1987). A mother cebus allowed her daughter to take sticks coated with syrup from her and to place a hand on her own hand during probing.

Restricting a discussion of tool use to the ontogeny of tool behavior in foraging is somewhat artificial. The study of these issues will advance only within the larger framework of the study of primate cognition and intelligence. An interesting perspective is offered by Parker and Gibson (1977, 1979), who classify tool use and suggest that certain types may correlate with extractive foraging. In their scheme, chimpanzees and cebus monkeys are the only intelligent tool users among primates. Specifically, they propose (1977:629) that "intelligent tool use correlates with extractive foraging on seasonally limited embedded foods and an omnivorous diet, while context specific tool use correlates with extractive foraging on nonseasonal embedded foods and a narrow non-omnivorous diet." The relationship of extractive foraging to tool use, food sharing, and information donation is explored in chapter 5.

The data reviewed in this chapter suggest two preliminary conclusions. First, primate immatures bear the primary responsibility for acquiring information from adults about foraging, whether with tools or without. This responsibility may involve some active behavior, and observational learning and imitation may not be as important as has long been assumed.

Second, when information donation does occur in foraging, a pattern is evident (whereas no pattern was found in information donation for social skills and predator avoidance). Active guidance of immature foraging skills is practiced more often in populations that share food and/or depend on foods whose preparation requires a long practice period. I suggest later that this relationship goes beyond the obvious fact that food sharing incorporates guidance of immature food choice; in addition, food sharing and reliance on extractive foraging may even select for increased information donation. Of course, other factors may be involved as well; correlation is not causation. In any case, before trying to *explain* any observed differences in social information transfer, primates other than monkeys and apes must be discussed.

4

HOMINIDS

A relationship long known to anthropologists from comparative anatomy—that humans are more closely related to monkeys and apes than to any other animals—has been clarified and elaborated in the last 20 years by new methods from molecular anthropology. These methods rely on the comparative analysis of genes and their constituents. They not only produce trees of relationships among species but also suggest the timing of certain species' divergence from common ancestors.

Two conclusions from molecular anthropology have particularly caught the attention of both the academic and the popular press. First, chimpanzees and humans shared a common ancestor as recently as 5 million years ago, and second, it is likely that humans are more closely related to chimpanzees than chimpanzees are to gorillas. These statements have been repeated so often that they may by now seem commonplace, but their significance is enormous—and for a human watching chimps and gorillas in a zoo, they may seem counter-intuitive. Our common ancestor with monkeys is more distant, but it is worth emphasizing that humans are more closely related to monkeys than to any other non-ape in the world.

Our close anatomical and genetic relationship with other primates has clear implications for the study of behavior. As discussed in chapter 1, research into monkey and ape behavior allows the identification of differences from and similarities with human behavior, which may then be studied using an evolutionary perspective. When behavioral differences are found—for example, in the use of teaching or speech to donate information to immatures—the tendency among some scientists may be to express awe at the unbridgeable gap in *behavior* that separates monkeys and apes from humans, despite the great physiological and genetic similarities between the two groups. Anthropologists are in a good position to comment on this seeming contradiction, because they have access (albeit in a frustratingly limited way) to the very creatures that can bridge the gap: hominids.

As Foley (1987:3) points out, behavioral differences between nonhuman and human primates seem so large partly because all intermediate beings are extinct. Chimpanzees and humans shared a common ancestor about 5 million years ago, but neither hominids nor humans evolved directly from apes, and so there are no "missing links" to be found. Rather, the term *intermediate* is meant to refer to hominids that evolved after the split with African apes but before the appearance of modern humans. The behavior of these hominids, if known, would likely make the "unbridgeable gap" between apes and modern humans appear less formidable to those for whom it looms large.

The problem for anthropological models is that the most appropriate comparison—extinct monkeys and apes with extinct hominids—cannot be made because the fossil record for extinct nonhuman primates is so limited. Instead, comparisons must be made between contemporary nonhuman primates and extinct hominids. Relethford (1990:242) summarizes what can be accomplished with this approach:

> The question of human uniqueness becomes more complicated when we consider possible behaviors of our fossil ancestors. Given a common ancestry with the African apes, at what point did our own patterns of toolmaking and language acquisition begin? Studies of modern apes help answer such questions because we can see the *potential* for such behaviors in the modern apes. Using these potentials as a guide to the behavior of the common ancestor of African apes and humans, we can attempt to determine what changes were necessary to arrive at the modern human condition.

This approach should, I believe, be broadened to include monkeys, particularly those from Africa and Asia (but see Snowdon 1990). As Steklis (1985: 168) notes, "When very few species are involved in the comparison (e.g., African apes and humans), there is a greater probability that any shared features were evolved independently and therefore may not have been present in a particular fossil ancestor. This is one reason why Old World monkeys are of great importance."

Understanding the evolution of primate behavior, including the behavior of hominids and humans, is the overall goal of many anthropologists who study primates, and it is mine as well. Although this chapter is devoted solely to hominids, in the next two chapters, information from all primates is integrated into a discussion of the evolution of social information transfer. The focus in this chapter is on the biological and archaeological evidence available to decode hominid behavior. Evidence from studies of the physiological capacity for hominid vocal communication, of hominid foraging, and of hominid material culture will be related to social acquisition and donation of information—sometimes, necessarily, in speculative ways.

Hominid Behavior: An Overview

Several textbooks in biological anthropology (e.g., Foley 1987; Relethford 1990; Campbell 1992) explain the biology of various hominid species and the possible phylogenetic relationships among them. Here I provide only the most basic foundation the nonanthropological reader will need to follow the discussion of social information transfer in hominids.

The hominid fossil record begins about 4 million years ago, with scrappy evidence going back perhaps another million years. The first hominids, the australopithecines, represent the point at which the known fossil record resumes after its limited representation of apes from about 10 million years ago. Between about 10 and 4 million years ago—precisely the time period in which evidence of the common ancestor of African apes and humans should be found—next to nothing is known about primate evolution. The fossil record thus virtually leaps from apes to hominids.

Australopithecines show dramatic changes in their method of locomotion when compared with the brachiating or knuckle walking of apes (again, one reason may be the lack of known intermediates). All australopithecines—there seem to be at least four species, but the number is debated—were bipedal. Although the exact form of this bipedalism is a subject of controversy, that australopithecines habitually walked upright and thus locomoted differently from any ape is undisputed. Whether australopithecines were totally committed to modern-type terrestrial bipedalism or, instead, occasionally used ape-type tree climbing *is* disputed (compare, e.g., Lovejoy 1988 with Susman et al. 1985). Paleoenvironmental reconstruction is important to this debate because the type of habitat available to australopithecines at around 4 million years ago shaped the selection pressures operating on their anatomy and behavior.

All known australopithecine remains have been found in sub-Saharan Africa, as were (and are) the African apes. Anthropologists have traditionally viewed extinct African apes as forest-dwelling brachiators and australopithecines as savanna-dwelling bipeds. Potts (1991a) asserts, however, that the notion of bipedalism as a savanna adaptation is based on logic rather than data. According to Potts, the best available data suggest that only about 2.5 million years ago did savanna significantly replace forest, well after the appearance of bipedal australopithecines. The earliest bipedalism may, in Potts's view, be interpreted as an attempt to preserve life in the forest as the distances between patches of food or shelter in the forest increased gradually before the savanna took over entirely. Bipedalism would have been selected for before commitment to the savanna occurred; early australopithecines would not have been savanna creatures.

If correct, this perspective has implications for models that focus on the consequences of early hominid adaptation to savanna foraging (Parker and Gibson 1979; Kurland and Beckerman 1985; and see chapter 5). The timing of replacement of forest by savanna is enormously important to understanding the evolution of both hominid anatomy and hominid behavior.

Although hard evidence is lacking for any sort of australopithecine behavior beyond bipedalism, some plausible reconstructive scenarios have been attempted, the best of which use data from chimpanzee studies to speculate about tool-use behavior in australopithecines (Tanner 1981, 1987; McGrew 1991). The logic is that knowledge of chimpanzees' capacities for tool use, tool modification, and other behaviors can indicate "the minimal capacity" for behavior of early hominids (McGrew 1991:13). Furthermore, anthropologists think that in brain size and organization (Falk 1992a), length of juvenile dependency (Bromage and Dean 1985; Bromage 1987), and, at least for some species, manipulative capability (Susman 1991), australopithecines were apelike.

Two million years after the start of the hominid fossil record, the first species appeared that is now classified as belonging to our own genus, *Homo.* Compared to australopithecines, *Homo habilis* shows increased brain size and brain reorganization (Tobias 1987; Falk 1992a). Modified stone tools are definitely associated with this species, as they are not with australopithecines (but see Susman 1991). The "cultural record" for hominids thus begins, so far as we know, with *Homo habilis.* The tools made by *Homo habilis* may, however, differ little from those of apes (Wynn and McGrew 1989; Potts 1991b). No evidence suggests that *Homo habilis* exhibited other cultural behaviors such as the use of semipermanent living sites, or home bases, control of fire, or group-organized foraging. The real innovation of this time period may involve not cultural factors as usually conceived but new patterns of resource use and the transport of raw materials over long distances (Potts 1991b).

Homo habilis was apparently replaced by a larger-brained hominid called *Homo erectus* at around 1.5 million years ago. *Homo erectus,* which lived for over a million years, colonized vast areas beyond Africa, spreading into Europe and Asia for the first time. Some anthropologists see in the archaeological evidence the use of semipermanent living sites, division of labor including big-game hunting, and control of fire by later populations of *Homo erectus.* The association of these behaviors with *Homo erectus* rather than *Homo sapiens* is controversial (see Binford 1989), but it is clear that a behavioral shift occurs with *Homo erectus.* This hominid shows far greater control over the environment than did earlier species. For the first time, hominids were adapted to cold climates as well as to the tropics; it seems likely that some kind of organized hunting would have been a prerequisite for such adaptation. Furthermore, significant shifts occurred in the manufacture of flake tools, such as those involving greater specialization of tool types for different tasks.

Homo sapiens sapiens—the term refers to anatomically modern humans and excludes all archaic forms of *Homo sapiens*—date to about 100,000 years ago and possibly earlier if dates from sites in South Africa (e.g., Border Cave) are confirmed (see Campbell 1992). Intermediates between late *Homo erectus* and early *Homo sapiens sapiens* exist but are not well described, and little is known of their behavior.

Patterns of descent from *Homo erectus* to *Homo sapiens sapiens,* including the relationship of Neandertals to both these species, are hotly contested in anthropology (for alternative interpretations of the evidence, see, e.g., Trinkaus 1989; Mellars and Stringer 1989). Neandertals, who lived approximately 75,000 to 32,000 years ago and thus coexisted with *H. s. sapiens,* show behavioral advances over earlier hominids, although a tendency to overinterpret (and romanticize) Neandertal behavior is evident in some publications. Other writers argue that reports of belief in an afterlife or even "the first religion" and of compassionate care of sick and injured group members are almostly certainly overinterpretations of the Neandertal evidence (Tappen 1985; Dettwyler 1991). Evidence better supports the deliberate burial of conspecifics by Neandertals, a practice never before seen in the archaeological record. Because of the uncertain evolutionary position of Neandertals, their behavior will not be discussed in detail.

Substantial agreement exists that a suite of new behaviors arose with *Homo sapiens sapiens.* Mellars (1991) discusses seven behavioral changes that occurred in Europe at around 40,000 years ago: replacement of flake tools by blade tools; imposition of increasingly standardized shapes and forms on tools; shaping of new substances, namely bone, antler, and ivory, in tool manufacture; regional diversification in behavior; appearance of personal ornaments; appearance of arts; and closely associated changes in economic and social organization, including specialized hunting and an increase in the density of human settlements. A similar package of behaviors has been labeled by Diamond (1992) as "The Great Leap Forward." Its timing at 40,000 years ago highlights the fact that the appearance of anatomically modern humans did not coincide with the appearance of behaviorally modern humans.

Hominids and Information: The Role of Speculation

Three points structure this discussion of social information transfer in hominids. First, behavioral developments related to social information transfer are correlated with broad time periods. Broadly tracing changes in hominids' opportunities and abilities, particularly those related to information donation, is more reliable than attempting to pinpoint precise dates for behavioral shifts. When patterns of broad change are envisioned, they are less likely to be made soon obsolete by new data. There is no guarantee, of course, that my interpretation of the evidence is the best one, only that it should be relatively robust against new data that may alter details of the proposed timing and sequence.

Second, my goal in this discussion is to support the general hypothesis that newly evolved behavior, intelligence, and technology allowed more information to be transferred from adults to immatures among hominids than among most primates. Chimpanzees and australopithecines may share features of information transfer, judging by other similarities in their behavior; thus the increase is meant in general terms, comparing most hominids to most primates. Part of the reason for such an increase might be that hominids transferred information in more behavioral contexts than do most other primates. For example, significant intergroup interaction, beyond avoidance, plays a role in hominid evolution but is conspicuously absent in nonhuman primates (Rodseth et al. 1991). Moreover, hominids used technology routinely and in a variety of contexts.

Third, and most significantly, because testing my general hypothesis is difficult with the limited data available, speculation must play a greater role in the discussion than I would prefer. Note that in wording the hypothesis, I predicted that more information *transfer* occurred in hominids. What I would like to say is that more information *donation* occurred. Although directed guidance, vocal communication, and teaching can be difficult to measure in primates, doing so is possible; in some cases it has been accomplished already, and in others, testable hypotheses can be imagined. For hominids, I am optimistic that anthropologists can study the general phenomenon of social information transfer but less hopeful about the chances for measuring directed information donation in prehistory. The ideal hypothesis to test would claim not only that hominids donated more information, but that the ratio of information acquisition to information donation shifted, with more information donation in hominids than information acquisition. But the possibilities for testing such a hypothesis seem limited, if they exist at all.

Scientists are constrained to speculate about hominid behavior not only by their obvious inability to observe hominids directly but also by the scarcity of fossil evidence. Insufficient fossil remains have been discovered even to allow complete or undisputed reconstruction of hominid anatomy, and the situation only becomes worse for the reconstruction of behavior. Foley (1989:28) notes that there are about 2,500 known fossil hominids from before 10,000 years ago, out of an estimated 5 billion hominids who must have lived between 8 million and 10,000 years ago. By this estimate, only about one in every 200 million hominids has been found so far—an extremely tiny "sample."

In assessing hominid social information transfer, it is important to use definitions that are clearly yet broadly devised, because they will allow the fullest use of the limited evidence for hominid behavior. From this perspective, Wobst's (1977:321) discussion of information in prehistory is the most useful. He includes as information exchange all "communication events in which a message is emitted or in which a message is received." Messages can be emitted in many different ways, not necessarily by vocal-auditory means. The challenge is to identify the potential message-sending abilities of hominids as reflected in their vocal and other social behavior and in their material culture.

This focus on message sending cannot target message sending to immatures. The term "information donation" can thus be used only in speculative reconstructions of hominid behavior. Neither does this focus allow full consideration of information acquisition or of the active roles adopted by hominid immatures in information acquisition. This shift in focus is inevitable, given the available data; admittedly, it is also a weakness of the diachronic approach.

To recap, my goal in this chapter is, ideally, to support the hypothesis that hominids donated more information to immatures than nonhuman primates do today—even if support can be offered only through speculative reconstruction. Closely related and perhaps more realistic goals are to show that there is (1) an increase in information transfer as one moves from consideration of most primates (excluding chimpanzees) to hominids, so that hominid behavior involved message sending more frequently than does primate behavior; and (2) an increase in information donation over the course of hominid evolution.

Vocal Communication

My choice of the comprehensive term *vocal communication* instead of "speech" is meant to make a point. Anthropologists too often equate the evolution of vocal production in hominids with the evolution either of modern speech alone or of gesture and modern speech together (but for important exceptions, see especially Steklis 1985; also Dibble 1989; Gibson 1991). More will be said in chapter 6 about the tendency to view speech and language as the watershed separating humans and other animals. For now, my point is simple. Most accounts—at least the ones that garner the most attention and get passed on to anthropology students—compare animal and human communication and then state or imply that before speech evolved, hominid vocal communication was primitive. This tendency stems from the assumption that all nonhuman primate vocalizations are involuntary, that is, not under the animal's conscious or neocortical control. Because it is wrong, this assumption and the conclusions to which it leads deserve serious examination.

Lieberman, a widely published and cited expert on the evolution of language, bases part of his newest book on the idea that "the evolution of the brain mechanisms that facilitate *voluntary* control of vocal communication is one of the keys to the evolution of human speech" (1991:74, emphasis in original). He dichotomizes nonhuman primate and human vocalizations, claiming that only the latter are voluntary, or under neocortical control (1991:21). Evidence to the contrary, however, has been in print for years and has been reviewed and synthesized as well. Steklis (1985:163) demolished any strict dichotomy between nonhuman and human vocalizations years ago:

> Recent evidence . . . shows that all monkey calls are not simply involuntary expressions regulated by subcortical structures. Rather, like human speech, monkey calls are complex structurally and functionally . . . which appears to be reflected at the level of governing neural mechanisms. Available evidence points not only to the existence of volitional components in calls but also the possible existence of a differentiation of neural mechanisms according to call type. Furthermore, as in speech, hemispheric asymmetries exist with regard to auditory analysis and perhaps also production of calls.

Lieberman takes the supposedly involuntary vocalizations of nonhuman primates as a starting point for the evolution of hominid vocal communication. Australopithecines, according to Lieberman, may have been unable to produce vocalizations other than in the context of gestural display, and may or may not have had voluntary control of speech. With *Homo erectus,* a major change in the vocal tract allowed "at least rudimentary voluntary speech motor ability" (Lieberman 1991:74).

Anthropology textbooks often cite Lieberman's writings and base their own scenarios about hominid communication on them. Campbell's account (1992:357) is typical in its suggestion that australopithecines, unlike nonhuman primates, may have been able to make "a few voluntary sounds." A gradual development in languagelike skills then followed, so that "by the time of *Homo erectus,* the rudiments of language might have appeared." Campbell (1992:356) explicitly characterizes nonhuman primates as incapable of voluntary vocalization: "We must conclude that primate vocalization did not evolve into language, which is clearly a volitional act. Instead, language is an entirely novel development in our evolution."

As Steklis (1985) pointed out, and as reviews of Lieberman's book reinforce (Falk 1992b; Gibson 1994), these scenarios do not square with the data from primatology (see also Cheney and Seyfarth 1990 for a description of voluntary vocal production in monkeys—e.g., how vervets vary calls according to context). The confusion may stem from the widespread assumption that chimpanzees cannot vocalize voluntarily or referentially. Goodall's view (1986) that most chimpanzee communication is emotional and involuntary is often cited in support of this assumption. For several reasons, taking her view as sufficient evidence for the involuntary nature of ape vocalizations is premature, as is using it to reach the kinds of conclusions asserted by Lieberman and Campbell.

First, because the relevant behavioral and neurophysiological research has not been performed on apes, no reliable conclusions can yet be drawn about voluntary versus involuntary, or referential versus emotional, communication in apes (Snowdon 1990). No playback experiments, for example, have been conducted at Goodall's or any other ape-research site. Second, experiments by Savage-Rumbaugh and her colleagues suggest that bonobos may be capable of voluntary vocalizations. Gibson (1991:260), after hearing audio-tapes of the bonobo Kanzi's vocalizations, reported that "he produced sounds astonishingly like those of the English words, 'carrot', 'snake' and 'right now.'" Kanzi's skills at comprehending spoken English are impressive (Greenfield and Savage-Rumbaugh 1990). Even if his utterances represent vocal mimicry, they would still constitute important data for any discussion of voluntary control of vocalizations by apes.

Furthermore, the ability of some monkeys to produce voluntary vocalizations is ignored when hominid vocal communication is discussed. Although no evidence exists either for or against voluntary vocal production in chimpanzees, it is known that some monkeys do produce calls voluntarily. Why, then, should the monkey evidence not be used to consider the possibility that early hominids were capable of referential vocal production? The problem cannot be a reluctance to speculate on the basis of nonhuman primate behavior, since scenarios of australopithecine tool behavior are based on that of chimpanzees. If an objection is that monkeys are not as closely related to humans as are chimpanzees, then Steklis's comment about the relevance of monkeys to the study of human evolution, quoted earlier, deserves renewed attention. What would happen to scenarios of hominid communication if apes were found to communicate in a way similar to that of vervets in their use of alarm calls?

The idea that australopithecines might have used referential vocal communication in more than a primitive way relies, indeed, only on evolutionary logic and is untestable. It does have the advantage, however, of being consistent with the data from primatology, as the assumption that all nonhuman primates vocalize involuntarily does not. Once this imaginary constraint on early hominid vocal production is removed, plausible scenarios may be constructed. As Gibson (1991:260) puts it: "Vocal symbolism could, of course, have arisen prior to modern phonemic capacities." Referential vocal communication and speech should be decoupled in reconstructive scenarios. Referential vocal communication about specific objects or events might well have been possible before speech evolved, just as it is possible for some nonhuman primates.

The evolution of modern speech should not be the only issue for anthropologists interested in vocal communication, but it is a fascinating one with potential to inform any discussion of social information transfer. Concerning the significance for human behavior of modern patterns of speech, Lieberman (1991) is convincing. Focusing on the reception and decoding, as well as the transmission, of human speech, he cites Miller's experiment of almost 30 years ago showing that humans are unable to identify incoming sounds at rates exceeding seven to nine items per second, with one major exception—speech. Speech is typically transmitted at about 15 to 25 sounds per second and is easily understood at that rate. As Lieberman (1991:37–38) points out, this high transmission rate is permitted by specific features of human physiology and is important because it allows long sentences (and hence complex thoughts) to be transmitted within the constraints of short-term memory. It would be useful to know when this ability to decode high-rate speech evolved, assuming that there is no necessary relationship between the timing of the development of production skills and that of comprehension skills. In the context of information transfer, it would seem that referential, voluntary communication would be selected for only to the extent that it was comprehensible to at least some members of the social group.

Most anthropologists, Lieberman included, study the evolution of speech by analyzing the evolution of vocal production, that is, of the vocal tract's physiology. Looking only at the vocal tract, the consensus (such as it is) suggests that physiological constraints would have prevented anything like human speech before the appearance of *Homo erectus*. The major constraint relates to the position of the larynx, which is too high in most mammals, including hominids before *Homo erectus*, to permit modern-type speech (for details see Lieberman 1991). The larynx, of course, is made of soft tissue and does not fossilize; computer modeling and reconstructions of hominid vocal tracts must be used in place of direct anatomical study. Although these methods seem to rule out any humanlike speech before *Homo erectus*, other data point to contradictory conclusions. Brain reorganization in *Homo habilis* indicates to some anthropologists (Tobias 1987; Falk 1992a) that speech was possible for that hominid.

The speech abilities of Neandertals have been particularly controversial. The debate was recently fueled by the discovery—the first ever in paleoanthropology—of a fossilized hyoid bone. Associated with a Neandertal dating to about 60,000 years ago, this hyoid suggests modern speech abilities to some anthropologists (Arensburg et al. 1990), but for others it is an unreliable indicator of speech (Lieberman 1991). Such a controversy is probably more important for understanding the long period of overlap between Neandertals and *Homo sapiens sapiens* than it is for illuminating the evolution of speech abilities in hominids. Overall, the most reliable conclusion at present seems to be that humanlike speech (although not referential vocal communication) was impossible for australopithecines, that it first developed at some time during the evolution of early *Homo,* and that in terms of rate, efficiency, and other features like syntax, it developed gradually (Steklis 1985; Greenfield 1991).

Data from primates and hominids suggest that the ability to send messages to conspecifics via referential vocal communication did not suddenly arise with modern speech, but evolved gradually. Rapid modern speech allows for more efficient transfer (and donation) of more information than does nonspeech vocal communication. But speech is not the only method of voluntary referential vocal communication. If, as suggested in this chapter, *Homo* donated more information to immatures than did early hominids or nonhuman primates, then referential vocal production, and eventually speech, would have been valuable supplements to other methods of guidance.

Foraging Behavior

Considering the conclusions reached in earlier chapters, it would be particularly helpful to know whether early hominids transferred information or sent messages to one another about social skills, predator avoidance, and foraging. Evidence is available only for the third of these categories, and even then is limited. Questions to be asked might focus on the intersection of foraging and social behavior: What can be reconstructed about the coordination and sharing of information in hominid foraging? When did high levels of voluntary, reciprocal food sharing arise? Did the types of food available have an effect on food sharing or social information transfer?

For almost a decade, the dominant behavioral model in paleoanthropology was Isaac's (1978). Isaac, an archaeologist, claimed that he had found evidence for "home bases," postponed consumption of food, and food sharing in East African hominids (most likely *Homo habilis*) at about 2 million years ago. According to Isaac, sites with mixed hominid tools and the bones of many animal species were home bases or semipermanent base camps, safe areas to which hominids would return after a day's foraging. Using ethnographic analogy—that is, fashioning a referential model with contemporary hunter-gatherer behavior as the foundation—Isaac suggested that hominid females would bring vegetable food, and hominid males, meat, back to the home base for exchange and sharing.

Other archaeologists (Potts 1988; Binford 1989) have powerfully challenged the claim that the archaeological evidence from 2 million years ago supports such a complex model of social behavior. The now-dominant paleoanthropological view doubts the antiquity of such humanlike behavior. Potts, for example, suggests that home bases would have endangered, rather than made safe, relatively defenseless early hominids such as *Homo habilis.* "Evidence for controlled use of fire, extensive destruction of bones that bear edible tissues, or exclusively hominid modification of bones (i.e., no carnivore modification) would indicate the presence of behaviors essential for home base activity" (Potts 1988:291). Such behaviors are not indicated for *Homo habilis* but probably appeared during the period of late *Homo erectus*.

To the extent that a home base implies the splitting up of foraging parties and their later reunion for food sharing, it carries implications for social information transfer, no matter when it first appeared. First, a home base suggests that the ability to discuss past encounters, future plans, and remote areas was more advantageous and selected for in hominids than in other primates (Isaac 1986). Second, it would have allowed some group members to remain at a fixed meeting place during the day. Such individuals could become caretakers for immatures who were past weaning age and thus no longer dependent on suckling for nutrition but who were still being provisioned by adults (Lancaster n.d.). Leisure time—or at least time not spent in the energetically costly periods of traveling to forage that constrain the time budgets of many primates—probably increased with the use of a home base; time available for adults to interact with and possibly donate information to immatures almost certainly increased. Third, a home base implies a commitment to voluntary, reciprocal food exchange beyond the level of mother-infant sharing that is found in some apes and presumably in early hominids as well. All together, a home base can be envisioned as a place where significant parent-juvenile and adult-adult food sharing occurred, and also as "a protected site for the spending of juvenile leisure time spent in play, object manipulation and the development of skilled performance created by food sharing between adults and young" (Lancaster n.d.).

In hominids living before the origin of home bases, food sharing between mothers and offspring was probably selected for, as it is in chimpanzees. It may have correlated with what Parker and Gibson (1979:373) term *tool-aided extractive foraging*: "During a long apprenticeship period, juvenile protohominids depended on their mothers and other close kin to share food with them, to help them open embedded foods, and to act as models for extractive foraging." Parker and Gibson (1979:371) see a shift to "primary year-round dependence on such tool-aided extractive foraging" as an explanation for hominid differentiation from the apes. Data from primatology and paleoanthropology can also be interpreted as showing no obvious differences between *some* apes and *some* early hominids in terms of tool use, extractive foraging, and food sharing. For this reason and others, an alternative to Parker and Gibson's interpretation, developed in chapter 5, suggests that tool-aided extractive foraging was important in some aspects of primate behavioral evolution but not in hominization per se (see also King 1986).

The important point for this discussion is that early hominid foraging may be viewed as an attempt to solve, probably with tools, a series of extractive foraging problems. Whether early hominids inhabited primarily savanna, woodland, or forest will prove important for this perspective, because food availability and perhaps the processing difficulty of food items may differ according to habitat. The typical view is that foraging in the savanna or savanna-woodland challenged early hominids and selected for greater intelligence and information exchange (e.g., Parker and Gibson 1979; Kurland and Beckerman 1985; and see Peters 1987 for a discussion of woodland foraging by some australopithecines). Hominid foraging is often described in ways that clearly indicate extractive-foraging abilities, even when the term itself is not used. The importance of underground plants to early hominids has been stressed by Hatley and Kappelman (1980:383):

> Belowground storage parts of water-edged plants and perennials of semiarid areas comprised a nutrient cache that was an integral part of the habitats of early hominids. The strategy of keying into a resource that was largely free from the effects of grazing, fire, and seasonal drought would assure a more reliable food source than that offered by above ground vegetation.

The three types of foods described by Isaac (1980) as exploited exclusively by human hunter-gatherers, or more intensively by humans than by nonhuman primates, are all in some way embedded foods that are hard to locate or process: hard-shelled nuts, meat from large animals, and underground tubers. Presumably, although not necessarily, the ability to exploit these foods or to exploit them more intensively than monkeys and apes developed during hominid evolution.

Dependence on extractive foraging, whether or not it was more developed in early hominids than in great apes, would have maintained high levels of selection for adult guidance of immature foraging. Early food sharing would likely have taken place primarily between mothers and offspring, as it does in other primates. Later, after the development of home bases, wider networks of food sharing probably formed. Food sharing would now be based not just on guiding immatures' use of those hard-to-process foods eaten by both mother and offspring, but also on differential foraging, possibly through a sexual division of labor (Isaac 1978). Immatures would acquire information along with the food items themselves. This interpretation of hominid foraging and food sharing, although speculative, is consistent with the suggestion that hominids donated more information than did other primates, and that information donation increased during human evolution.

Material Culture

The third context to be assessed for social information transfer and message sending in hominids demands the greatest degree of speculation. Some artifacts, including tools and art, may carry messages unrelated to their function. The idea that messages can be sent through material culture is far from new; it has been discussed by archaeologists as the concept of style for almost 20 years.

Different archaeologists define style in different ways (e.g., Wobst 1977; Conkey 1978; papers in Conkey and Hastorf 1990). The clearest definitions share an emphasis on the use of material culture to communicate about social identity or available resources. Rice (1987:244), for instance, considers style to be contained in "visual representations, specific to particular contexts of time and place," that transmit information about the identity of the society in question and about the situation or location involved. Wiessner makes the point that the process of identity formation is important in understanding style; she emphasizes this aspect in her definition of style as nonverbal communication about relative identity (1990:107).

Either social differentiation or social cohesion may be emphasized in theories that discuss the role of style in behavior. According to Wiessner, the need to establish and project a positive, individualistic self-image is basic to humans. This need may be exacerbated in the face of increasing population density, when "individuals often feel the need to distinguish themselves from others and to express greater individuality" (Wiessner 1990:109). On the other hand, as population size and the number of social groups increase, the need for social cohesion within each group may also increase. Whether the emphasis is on cohesion or differentiation would seem to be a matter of focus and scope; that is, whether the focus is within a single group or between groups, within a network or between networks, and so forth.

It would be unwise to make any assumptions about the psychological needs of hominids. Instead, views of hominid material culture that attribute social-identity functions to style share the basic assumption that artifacts such as tools and art can carry messages about abstractions such as mutually expectable behavior patterns (Wobst 1977:327) and about the ways a community organizes and categorizes its perceptions (Rice 1987:251). What sometimes remains ambiguous is precisely *how* tools or art could achieve social cohesion (Conkey 1987:422) or enhance social differentiation.

The underlying philosophy that binds together these assumptions, and that accompanies a search for style in material culture, has been made explicit by Gero (1989). She notes that the traditional archaeological view of artifacts and their makers is "curiously passive," and then proposes another perspective:

Alternatively, the makers of prehistoric artifacts can be seen in an active mode, as very purposeful actors who can use material culture not merely to subsist but also to form, maintain, and transform social relationships. Here, material culture is manipulated to display social symbols in appropriate contexts, to underwrite ethnic unity or to press personal advantage. . . . It is possible to identify a set of characteristics relevant for all material objects that seems to determine how much and what kind of a role a particular item might play in transmitting social information. (Gero 1989:92–93; see also the discussion of active versus passive style in Sackett 1990)

Gero's archaeological research in Peru covers the period from 2000 BC to 600 AD. Can her perspective—which she credits as originating with Wobst (1977)—be applied to hominids? Can style, if it exists in hominid material culture, help us understand social information transfer? These questions are best addressed through specific cases in which material culture associated with certain hominids has been examined for function and possible meaning. As examples, I will discuss tools made by early hominids and art produced by *Homo sapiens sapiens.*

That hominid tools might be studied for what they tell us about their makers is a perspective embraced by some archaeologists and challenged by others. The first known hominid tools, termed *Oldowan,* are those manufactured primarily by *Homo habilis* (but see Susman 1991). No archaeologist, to my knowledge, argues for style in Oldowan tools, of which only a few types exist. These unifacial tools seem relatively multipurpose in function and simple to manufacture. Recently a psychologist and a primatologist collaborated to suggest that a comparison of Oldowan and ape tools shows no significant cognitive-based differences between them (Wynn and McGrew 1989). One behavioral difference is that Oldowan toolmakers used some tools to produce others, which no ape in the wild has done (Kitahara-Frisch 1993) (although a captive bonobo, Kanzi, can do this with relatively limited human guidance; see Toth et al. 1993). Nonetheless, the first important changes from ape to hominid tools apparently came about only with the tools made primarily by *Homo erectus,* which are termed *Acheulean.*

Acheulean tools, like so much else in biological anthropology, are at the core of a debate. It is accepted that there are more types of Acheulean than Oldowan tools, and that the manufacture of bifacial tools such as the Acheulean handax is more complex. But to some anthropologists (e.g., Isaac 1986; Wynn 1989, 1991), Acheulean tools show evidence of arbitrary, imposed form. As Wynn (1989:97–98) puts it:

In order for several hominids to have manufactured tools with the same shape, they must have shared some idea about what was appropriate and what was not. This is especially true when, as in the case of the biface, there is no overriding functional reason for the shape, which is essentially arbitrary.... Perhaps for the first time, we can talk about a hominoid's behavior in terms of shared, arbitrary standards.

Wynn dates the advent of arbitrary forms and shared community standards to 1.2 million years ago, squarely during the time period for *Homo erectus.*

If Wynn's views are accepted, what might they mean for hominid social information transfer? One interpretation is that a shared community standard within a *Homo erectus* group would require a considerable degree of communication among its members and, likely, information donation to immatures. If shared ideas and community standards varied between groups, then style could have functioned to indicate group membership or maintain group boundaries. In this case, immatures would have had to acquire the information necessary for producing tools that both carried the correct group-specific messages and were made correctly to serve their intended function. Shared standards might then have been important enough or complex enough to require direct guidance or teaching of immatures by adults. Alternatively, the level of standardization adopted by *Homo erectus* groups in tool manufacture might have been acquired entirely through observational learning (see Conkey 1978) or some other form of information acquisition. Some archaeologists (e.g., Conkey 1978) suggest that only with later hominids, such as Neandertals, does standardization reach levels that point to shared ideas.

Whereas some archaeologists debate the timing of the appearance of arbitrary, imposed form in hominid tools, others, particularly Dibble (1987, 1989; Chase and Dibble 1987) raise serious challenges to the assumption underlying the debate itself. Dibble's main point is that any morphological patterning in hominid tools for the time period of *Homo erectus* and Neandertal is due to basic technological factors, not to the imposition of arbitrary form and shared standards. A major source of typological variation is the "continuous reduction of the pieces through resharpening and remodification until their eventual discard" (Dibble 1989:417). Dibble's own research on hominid scrapers reinforces the view that tools were continuously reworked until they were thrown away. In turn, any standardization found in such tools would not necessarily reflect meaningful categories for the hominids who made them (Dibble 1989:427). These tools may not, after all, have sent messages in the way conceived of by the proponents of style, and therefore the kind of information donation that might be selected for by information-loaded tools may not have existed.

If Dibble is right, does it mean that information acquisition alone is likely to have been sufficient for obtaining knowledge about tool manufacture? The debate about style and standardization may be more significant for consideration of the origins of language and symbolism than it is for social information transfer. Dibble points out that tool manufacture by all species involves the imposition of form; the important question is whether that form is arbitrary. Although he believes that arbitrary form has not yet been demonstrated in hominid tools before the Upper Paleolithic, Dibble notes that certain features of the tools do vary. Thus

> it could be argued that inter- and intra-regional variations in technology or the choice of raw material—the factors that have been shown here to be fundamental—represent different "isochrestic" styles that reflect different ethnic groups. But such technological traditions reflect the fact that tool making is a learned behaviour and one that was transmitted within the social group. Now, the tools of the Lower and Middle Palaeolithic are clearly much more complicated than anything produced by non-human primates. . . . But like many other learned behaviours in primates, there is nothing in these kinds of technologies that necessarily forces us to assume a linguistic mode of transmission. (Dibble 1989:427)

Dibble's point is compatible with one of the themes of this book, which is developed fully in the final chapter. Many behaviors that involve social information transfer do not require linguistic transmission; there are many other ways to guide immatures' behavior. Young hominids may have been guided by adults in tool manufacture whether or not the tools sent messages about social identity according to shared community standards. In short, within-group standardization of tool manufacture, along with cross-group variation in standardization, seems the most likely context in which to search for style and information donation—which may, however, have required a degree of regional differentiation that did not appear until the time of *Homo sapiens sapiens.*

Shifting the focus to hominid art, a similar lack of consensus as that for the study of tools can be noted among archaeologists. Saying that the function of Paleolithic artwork is open to interpretation is an understatement. As Conkey (1987) notes, the term "Paleolithic art" lacks meaning because it collapses all diversity and invites single-cause theories of what the art might mean. The art dates to between 25,000 and 10,000 years ago, is restricted to Europe, and includes portable artifacts such as sculptures, engravings, and decorated tools as well as paintings, engravings, and sculptures on the walls of caves and rockshelters (Jochim 1983).

One position (Halverson 1987) is that the art has no particular meaning, reference, or social usage, including anything related to social information transfer. Another takes the view that the relatively sudden appearance of art in human evolution (but see Marshack 1989) is not directly related to increasing intelligence or brain evolution but rather is a response to handling more and different types of information (e.g., Gamble 1983:522). Two broad types of interpretation within the information-transfer perspective have received the most attention.

In one interpretation, art helps to cement processes of social identification within or between groups. Archaeologists point out that Paleolithic art is found disproportionately in stressful environments such as harsh northern latitudes where resource availability would likely be unpredictable (Gamble 1983) and shared information would reduce risk. If art is produced according to some shared standard, it may reduce the stress of repeated interactions between groups not in constant verbal contact (Wobst 1977), and may in turn strengthen avenues of communication and affiliation (Jochim 1983). These theories and others like them differ in detail but share a certain view of Paleolithic society:

> Rather than viewing Upper Paleolithic hunters and gatherers in southwestern Europe as members of the tiny, isolated "band" formations of the basic model, these scholars envision them as integrated into vast regional networks, emphasizing marriage ties, information exchange, and social and religious interaction. . . . By facilitating the sharing of both information and risk, these regional networks are seen as contributing directly to the adaptive success of the peoples of southwestern Europe. (Mueller-Wille and Dickson 1991:48)

Although the kinds of theories just mentioned sometimes explain only vaguely the actual mechanisms by which art contributes to information transfer (Conkey 1987), in some cases real precision is offered. Among the more well-conceived interpretations is Davidson's (1989), which speculates about the function of plaquette art in Spain during the Upper Paleolithic. Plaquettes are stone artifacts on which pictures have been painted, engraved, or both. Davidson's research was carried out at the site of Parpallo, where over six thousand such pieces were found; it is the only site in eastern Spain with abundant plaquettes. Clumped distribution of plaquettes is the norm in western Europe, according to Davidson. This fact, taken together with other data on the spatial distribution of art in the region, indicates to Davidson the presence of only a few "territories" in that part of the world at that time. He bases his idea that plaquette art played an active role in information transfer on reconstructions of seasonally differentiated foraging behavior:

Human groups which dispersed seasonally for the exploitation of particular resources having a short period of availability might have needed some mechanism to ensure the aggregation of the group at other seasons. . . . Plaquette "art" sites were clearly exceptional within a group of related sites, and activities at them clearly included both domestic and ritual. At such sites, regularly visited over long periods, and through "cultural" changes, information and genes may have been shared. In this way the rights and rites of the territorial group would be reproduced. (Davidson 1989:451)

Davidson's ideas are intriguing for two reasons. They suggest, first, a precise role for art in information transfer, and second, that information may have been restricted as well as shared during the Paleolithic. Data about plaquette distribution suggest that the few existing territories involved "social hierarchies which retained their control over these centres of association" (Davidson 1989:452). As Davidson points out, even a single information system might be composed of three different aspects, each of which has been emphasized by different archaeologists: ideas may have been held in common by a whole society (Davidson credits Gamble here); ideas may have been distributed differentially in a group, but with common sharing of ideas when the group aggregated (Davidson credits Conkey here); and ideas may have been available only under conditions of restricted access to information (Davidson's own interpretation; 1989:452).

Within the context of social information transfer, the same questions asked about hominid tools could be asked about the supposed "social identification" function of art—particularly those questions focusing on the role of within-group versus between-group variation and on what information immatures needed to acquire about material culture. Information donation itself cannot be assumed from any of the theories about the role of art in social identity or social cohesion. Clearly, however, material culture provides an important potential avenue for message sending even at the relatively late date by which hominid art first appeared, when vocal-auditory communication, including speech, was presumably sophisticated.

In the second approach to Paleolithic art from an information-transfer perspective, art provides information for decision making about resources. The role of art itself is more straightforward here, and a clear role for information donation is more easily imagined. Nonportable art, such as cave paintings, might function to direct the attention of immatures or teach skills related to selective attention; that is, it might help immatures learn how to learn and how to gather information for decision making by, for example, focusing their attention on the most salient features of the environment (Pfeiffer 1982;

Mithen 1988:322). Information about the environment transferred through art, whether to immatures or other adults, may be quite specific; Mithen (1988) notes that Paleolithic images include marks that may depict the footprints or tracks associated with various prey species.

All in all, the analysis of style as a means of social information transfer is on stronger ground when applied to art than to early hominid tools. By the time art appears, during the Upper Paleolithic, regional differentiation of behavior and increased population density are also in evidence (Mellars 1991). Modern-type speech capacities were probably in place as well, along with multiple examples of information-loaded material culture. By studying material culture, anthropologists derive another window into message sending, one that looks beyond the vocal-auditory channel.

Support for the hypothesis that the rate of message sending in hominids increased compared to that in other primates, and increased over the time span of human evolution, comes from three areas. First, the evolving hominid brain and vocal tract point to increasing ability to produce referential signals vocally, even before modern speech. Using new data on the voluntary, referential vocalizations of nonhuman primates to form "minimum-standard models" is particularly important in arguing this point.

Second, what we know about hominid foraging suggests that tool-aided extractive foraging continued to be as or more important in early hominids than in chimpanzees. Food sharing, and thus guidance of immature foraging, was probably a part of this behavioral package. Food sharing and information donation may have increased in quantity and quality at the time when home bases appeared. Home bases imply that appropriate time and space were available for adults to interact with and possibly guide their young; they also imply more extensive food sharing than that of mothers and offspring.

Third, the analysis of material culture suggests that hominid art and possibly some tools sent messages unrelated to their function. Messages might have been sent about social identity or food resources to other individuals or other groups, possibly including immatures; immatures might have needed tutoring in the production as well as the comprehension of those messages. The role of information donation in hominid material culture, however, remains speculative.

Because information donation itself can be discussed only speculatively, the major conclusion has to be that message sending increased in hominids compared to other primates. I strongly suspect that information donation did as well. Challenges to this view might come from future study; the abilities of monkeys, apes, or early hominids to donate information might be found to have been underestimated, for example, or speculation about hominid behavior might be proven wrong. But at present, *Homo erectus* seems to represent a kind of turning point for information donation among hominids. By this I mean not a qualitative difference or leap but rather a shift in degree, and a particularly noticeable one according to the available evidence. This shift may be similar in degree to the one seen between chimpanzees and other nonhuman primates.

Shifts in the abilities underlying referential vocal communication, complex foraging, and the production of sophisticated technology and art have their roots in physiology, including neurophysiology. The brain of *Homo habilis* seems to be markedly more humanlike than the brains of australopithecines (Tobias 1987; Falk 1992a), and changes in brain size and organization, of course, continued throughout human evolution. Some scholars (e.g., Gibson 1990, n.d.; Greenfield 1991) have produced scenarios linking hominids' behavioral advances with specific changes in the evolving brain. The relationship between evolving cognition and evolving donation of information will be discussed in the next chapter.

5

A DIACHRONIC MODEL FOR
INFORMATION DONATION

A thorough discussion of social information transfer in primates must include modern humans. In keeping with the subjects treated in earlier chapters, my goal in the first part of this chapter is to support the contentions that human adults actively donate information to immatures in a variety of contexts and that human infants are excellent information acquirers who may influence their own socialization (see also King n.d.). From there, I will go on to suggest a framework for assessing social information transfer diachronically—that is, for analyzing changes over time in information acquisition relative to information donation in primates.

Social Information Transfer in Humans

Surprisingly few anthropologists have tested hypotheses to find out if human children acquire certain skills, and the information upon which those skills depend, primarily through information donation or information acquisition. The best clues to this issue come from hints about the training or teaching of children that are scattered throughout ethnographies and articles about child socialization. Anthropologists seem to take teaching in humans for granted, so they fail to study it empirically or they prefer to emphasize more subtle influences on child development, as Whiting and Whiting (1975) do in their classic cross-cultural study.

One anthropological approach to social information transfer in humans would investigate how the information needed to master certain skills was acquired by immatures in a variety of cultures. Attempting to untangle the role of verbal instruction from other types of teaching would be a good place to start.

Perhaps a child must master the skills necessary for digging up underground tubers, an extractive foraging task. Only certain tools made in certain ways will get this job done efficiently, and only certain tubers found in re- stricted locations are edible and nutritious. Assuming that social information transfer occurs—rather than simply trial and error without any social inter- action—what is its nature? Do adults merely extract their own tubers while tolerating close observation and scrounging of food scraps by immatures? Or do adults guide immatures in their tool choice, tool modification, choice of location in which to search for tubers, or selection of tubers? Is this guid- ance primarily verbal or nonverbal? If primarily verbal, could the task have been learned in the absence of speech? If primarily nonverbal—that is, ac- complished through guidance of motor patterns—could the task have been learned through speech alone? Long-term observations in the child's natural habitat rather than in the laboratory would be most advantageous for answer- ing such questions, but complementing natural observations with controlled experiments in the natural setting would be ideal.

We know that human immatures attain some specific skills through di- rect training, verbal and otherwise. When considering the training of children, the notion of behavioral routines that are constructed by adults and directed toward immatures comes up repeatedly in the literature on child socialization and language acquisition. Parents among the Kipsigis of Kenya, for example, deliberately and methodically teach their infants to sit and walk: "There were specific behavioral routines, with specific words to refer to them, that parents and siblings all knew and practiced on a nearly daily basis months before the skills were fully acquired by the baby" (Super and Harkness 1986:556).

When focusing on how children acquire language skills, the idea be- hind the role of behavioral routines is that children learn language in the pro- cess of interacting with others in patterned ways (Bruner 1983; Peters and Boggs 1986:80; Tomasello 1992; Savage-Rumbaugh et al. 1993). In the con- text of verbal exchanges, "an *interactional routine* is a *sequence of exchanges* in which one speaker's utterance, accompanied by appropriate nonverbal be- havior, calls forth one of a limited set of responses by one or more other participants" (Peters and Boggs 1986:81, emphasis in original). In reviewing research on language acquisition in children, Parker (1985:618) points out that "mothers provide simple, repetitive stereotyped behavioral routines . . . that elicit, support, and organize the emerging communicative behaviors of their infants. By overestimating their infants' communicative intentions, mothers assign them a real interactional role and 'pull' them along the leading edge of their emerging abilities."

The mutual participation of adults and infants in this process is clear (see Bruner 1983), but the routines and interactions involved need not always be verbal (Bruner 1983; Tomasello 1988). Joint attentional processes may instead involve manipulating or exploring a toy in repeated and predictable ways. Or the adult may use a combination of verbal and nonverbal markers to highlight the predictability of everyday interactions with the infant:

> These routines scaffold the initial language acquisition of the child in the sense that they create, with no need of a conventional language whatsoever, a shared referential context within which the language of the adult makes sense to the prelinguistic child. And even after they have learned some words, children continue to acquire the vast majority of their language inside nonlinguistically understood joint attentional episodes. (Tomasello 1992:70)

Such a shared focus, when developed naturally, can be more effective for a child's language acquisition than the situation in which an adult explicitly directs the child's attention (Tomasello 1988).

Even when anthropologists do not mention behavioral routines, their descriptions of the training of children clearly indicate information donation, even to very young children. Among the Aka Pygmies of Zaire, children as young as 6 to 12 months of age are trained by their parents in subsistence skills involving small knives, axes, and spears (Hewlett 1991a). The amount of correction or punishment of children's behavior varies, of course, across cultures. The old anthropological generalization that adults in nonindustrial cultures are "indulgent" toward children is simplistic (Hewlett 1991b). Direct guidance, including correction and punishment, exists in many behavioral contexts in nonindustrial cultures.

In many societies, children are assigned certain tasks, sometimes according to gender; this kind of task assignment qualifies as a form of information donation because it directly guides immatures' experience and obtaining of knowledge. Extensive information donation exists in the context of feeding. Dettwyler (1989) notes the wide variety of techniques used cross-culturally by parents and other caretakers to control young children's food consumption, including force-feeding, physical punishment, physical restraint during eating, encouragement, feeding games, and rewards.

Judging from comparative data, the imitative ability of human immatures exceeds that of monkey and ape immatures (see Meltzoff 1988; Tomasello 1990; Visalberghi and Fragaszy 1990; Whiten and Ham 1992). Even so, for human children to acquire some knowledge may require (rather than merely benefit from) information donation. What sort of knowledge falls into this category is not known, but Gibson's (1991) distinction between techniques and technology in human tool use and manufacture may indicate where to look.

Technique, a type of procedural knowledge, involves a set of specific sensorimotor skills and action sequences, whereas technology, a type of declarative knowledge, is far more comprehensive. Technology involves "accumulated knowledge encompassing mathematical and scientific principles as well as information about the geographic, biotic, physical and social environments in which tools are made and used" (Gibson 1991:256). Gibson notes that language may have little influence on technique but profound influence on technology. Whereas techniques *may* be mastered through information acquisition alone (but would benefit greatly from information donation, as do the tool techniques of immature Tai chimpanzees), I suspect that skills related to technology require some kind of guidance, whether mediated through language or not. The logic here is reminiscent of that used earlier when I suggested that knowledge about hominid tool manufacture itself might be gained through information acquisition, but if tools also carry stylistic messages, then immatures would need information donation to master the broader implications of tool design. This argument may be extended to foraging because so much of human foraging is tool aided.

Information donation need not come from parents but may involve older siblings or other older children who have more experience or greater skills. Studying the effect of peer groups (which, despite the name, include children of different ages and experience levels) on child socialization "reverses a long-standing bias in western psychology that overemphasized the role of parents, especially the mother, as socialization agents" (Harkness and Super 1985:219). Within peer groups, gender segregation may not be enforced, but children tend to associate preferentially with members of their own sex, thus influencing their own socialization (Harkness and Super 1985) and acquiring information in a way reminiscent of behavior seen among some primates. These multi-age play groups "assist parents in childcare, help in the transmission of culture, and promote greater intergenerational equality" (Hewlett 1991b:18), and thus may involve information donation.

As a rule, nonindustrial societies exhibit a higher level of multiple caregiving to immatures than is seen in industrialized countries. In a quantitative study of this phenomenon among the Aka Pygmies, Tronick et al. (1987, cited in Hewlett 1991b) found unusually high levels of multiple caretaking: at four months of age, infants spent 60 percent of their time with people other than their mothers and were exchanged among caretakers over eight times per hour. Females other than the infant's mother often nursed the baby. A great deal of information presumably can be donated by nonparents in this context.

In recent years, interest has increased in the active, skilled human infant, a focus that—just as in the study of other primates—helps to counter the established focus on adults in socialization. This perspective can be applied productively even to the youngest infants. After years of working with neonates, Brazelton (1979:79) comments that "the old model of thinking of the new-born infant as helpless and ready to be shaped by his environment prevented us from seeing his power as a communicant in the early mother-father-infant-interaction." Brazelton's observation helps us envision the infant as capable of flexible behavior that elicits caretaking from adults, but it is hard to know whether or when the very young infant is actively gathering information or attending to parental cues transmitted verbally or nonverbally.

Attending to nonverbal behavior is an important way in which immatures acquire information from adults. Investigators study what is termed *social referencing* in order to explore the way in which immatures make use of adults' nonverbal cues, including facial expressions. In social referencing, infants use the expressive behavior of others to form their own emotional reactions (Feinman 1985). It may occur with or without solicitation—that is, the child might or might not actively solicit information by expressing some need. Examples of social referencing provide interesting parallels with the behavior of primates. A child may decide how to react to a strange person or object, for example, only after first checking with its mother by decoding her facial expression.

In the study of human social information transfer, then, information donation is known from a variety of behavioral contexts, but the precise relationship between information donation and information acquisition is not well understood. Still, it is evident that humans donate more information to immatures than do other primates. Structured behavioral routines are seen more frequently in humans than in other primates, although such routines may occur in other species as well, since they may be carried out either with or without language (see chapter 6). Like the young of their nearest relatives, human immatures are superb information acquirers, but even so the relative contributions of adults and immatures to information transfer shifts in humans (King n.d.). This result would be unsurprising if information donation were equated with verbal instruction, but it holds true even when, as in this book, no such equation is made. Adults in all human cultures practice guidance, correction, and teaching of immatures' behavior. The difference between humans and other primates is one of degree.

A Move Beyond Description

The comparison of data on the behavior of extant monkeys and apes with that for extinct hominids has suggested differences among primates in the relative roles played by immatures and adults in acquiring and donating information. Interpretation of patterns in these data can be made along two primary dimensions, phylogeny and behavioral context. Assessing social information transfer according to phylogeny produces a continuum of abilities related to information donation, but variation according to behavioral context appears to be significant as well.

Immature monkeys are adept at acquiring information about social skills, predators, and foraging by initiating and maintaining interactions with adults and by attending to cues made available to them through adult behavior. They receive donations of information from adults only rarely. An exception occurs in the foraging context among callitrichids, the only monkeys that regularly share food. Although skill at information acquisition is not lost in other primates, information donation increases along a continuum from monkeys to apes, hominids, and humans. Among great apes, especially the chimpanzee, information transfer in social skills and predator avoidance does not differ appreciably from that of monkeys. Information donation in foraging and in food sharing both increase, however, a correlation that may go beyond the simple fact that food sharing is a type of information donation; chimpanzees share more food than any other primate except callitrichids and donate more information about foraging in other ways as well. A pattern therefore emerges in the behavioral context of foraging, whereas no pattern is evident for information donation about social skills and predators.

Reconstruction of hominid social skills and predator avoidance is not currently possible, but reconstruction of hominid vocal communication, foraging strategies, and material culture suggests that hominid adults donated more information to immatures than do the adults of any other primates except modern humans. Early hominids—the australopithecines and *Homo habilis*—may have functioned similarly to chimpanzees in terms of foraging-related information donation. Increases in information donation occurred gradually, so that with *Homo erectus* and *Homo sapiens,* more information was donated more efficiently and probably in more contexts as well. The behavior of hominid young is particularly hard to assess, but presumably these immatures were efficient, active information gatherers, as are other primates. Adult donation of information nonetheless increased over time and culminated in the direct guidance and intentional teaching that characterizes modern human behavior.

Understanding why these behavioral changes came about can be undertaken within the framework of diachronic anthropology. Diachronic studies go beyond the description of behavior observed during selected "slices of time" to model change in biocultural systems. One drawback to the diachronic approach used here is that although I attempt to trace behavioral change using an evolutionary perspective and to look at the continuum of behavior across primate species, my method inevitably assumes that behavior observable in the present reflects behavior of the past.

Extant monkeys and apes can be compared to modern humans along a very real, observable behavioral continuum. Once hominids are included, however, the implication is that the behavior of extant monkeys and apes can stand in for the behavior of extinct monkeys and apes to produce a continuum in *time,* allowing the consideration of why certain behaviors originated, were selected for, and evolved. Problems with this approach are reminiscent of those associated with referential models (see chapter 1). The approach is most valuable when the aim is not to produce a referential model but rather to identify selection pressures that probably operated on past primate behavior and to create hypotheses that can be tested to further understand primate behavior in the present.

Two important points form the core of my diachronic approach. First, chimpanzees donate more information than do monkeys and other apes, although the difference is not one of kind but of degree. Indeed, chimpanzees are not obviously distinct from early hominids in terms of information donation. Second, the clearest pattern for information donation is found in the foraging context and correlates with food sharing and extractive foraging with tools. Because they are based on limited data, these points are better thought of as working hypotheses than as conclusions.

My goal now is to consider whether these two points can be *explained* as well as described using an evolutionary perspective. A few caveats must be offered. First, my focus is not on the evolution of the *capacity* for information donation; some monkeys are capable of it, as we have seen. Instead, the discussion converges on one question: Why is there increased information donation, especially during foraging, in chimpanzees and early hominids as compared to monkeys and other apes? Restricting my framework in this way is preferable to attempting a premature explanation of variation across behavioral contexts. Gaps in the data—for example, in our understanding of referential vocal communication in apes—are too large to permit reasonable speculation about variation across contexts. Moreover, a focus on foraging is particularly amenable to a continuum analysis because reconstructions of hominid foraging behavior are possible.

Second, with this restricted framework I admittedly risk asking the "wrong" questions. If the patterns I identify in the data do not hold up, the diachronic approach pursued here may go off in a direction that will not help anthropologists to understand change. Certainly a host of other questions emphasizing different aspects of behavior could be asked. I intend to suggest only one way in which diachronic anthropology might be applied to the issue of social information transfer.

Ultimate and Proximate Factors

Both ultimate and proximate factors may be important in the expression of increased information donation. Ultimate factors select for or "drive" the evolution of increased information donation. A focus on ultimate factors essentially asks how and why increased information donation evolved. A focus on prox-imate factors asks what immediate conditions allowed or encouraged the ex-pression of the capacity for information donation, and it includes consideration of the physiological and cognitive mechanisms of information processing.

Immediately it should be clear that keeping ultimate and proximate fac-tors distinct will be difficult at times. In the section on tool use in chapter 3, for example, some primates, including orangutans and gorillas, were shown to use tools only in captivity. Moving an orangutan from its natural habitat in southeast Asia to the National Zoo in Washington does not, of course, cause the capacity for tool use to appear. Nothing can be learned about the origin of tool use (the ultimate cause) by studying zoo orangutans, whereas much can be learned in the zoo setting about what proximate factors—perhaps leisure time or boredom (see Beck 1980)—encourage the expression of tool use. Prima-tologists know more about tool use in wild as opposed to captive primates than they do about capacity versus performance in information donation. Might monkeys that show limited information donation but clearly have the capacity for it become consistent information donors under certain circumstances? If so, the increased information donation claimed for chimpanzees would be a matter of proximate "releasers" and not ultimate factors.

Foley (1991:30) makes a distinction between conditions and phenotypic characters that should be maintained when trying to understand behavior:

> Conditions constitute the context or selective pressure that prompts or requires complex behaviour. Phenotypic characters are the actual behavioural characteristics that are selected for and come to be in-corporated in the behavioural repertoire, resting in the individual and providing it with a reproductive advantage.

In Foley's terms, then, I want to understand the conditions that led to in-creased information donation. My primary focus is on ecological conditions that affected foraging in primates. Certain cognitive abilities—phenotypic characters—must underlie increased information donation, and I explore one possible relationship between cognitive changes and information donation. Through a focus on ecology and a brief look at cognition, I examine increased information donation at one particular "shift point" in primate evolution—the shift to increased information donation that occurs in chimpanzees and early hominids as compared to monkeys and other apes. Use of the term *shift point* is not meant to suggest rigid stages of primate behavior. To assume a monkey stage, an ape-and-early-hominid stage, and a later hominid stage of behavior would be to misread seriously the intent of a gradualistic, diachronic approach. In fact, some populations of monkeys may behave in the ways ascribed to apes, some early hominids may fit better into the description for later hominids, and so on. Nevertheless, discussion of the primate continuum is most valuable, in my view, when it focuses on selected shift points.

Ecology and Cognition at the Shift Point

Ecological factors are all the features of an organism's habitat that affect its behavior, including climate, disease, predators, and food. My focus on food and foraging strategies does not imply that other ecological factors did not play a role in increased information donation. Cognition may be taken to mean the ability to relate previously unrelated pieces of information in novel ways and to apply the results to new problems (Markl 1985). Recent data and interpretations suggest that ecology and cognition may interrelate in significant ways. The cognitive abilities of primates may correlate with certain types of foraging strategies, such as frugivory or, more specifically, searching for fruit that is patchily distributed (Clutton-Brock and Harvey 1980; Milton 1981).

Although it may be possible eventually to treat them in a related way, I consider ecology and cognition separately here. Great apes, for example, may be able to behave in a cognitively more sophisticated way than most monkeys, yet ecological pressures may play a role such that monkeys adapted to certain environments may cognitively outperform most apes. Correlating cognition with phylogeny and ecology is neither original nor highly speculative, although alternative views exist (MacPhail 1987).

The thesis of my diachronic approach is this: a likely selection pressure for greater donation of information is a shift to dependence on foods that require a significant investment by immatures in acquiring foraging skills and the information on which those skills depend. Embedded foods that require extractive foraging with tools provide the best example. Extractive foraging and its significance for primate evolution has been explored in a series of papers by the anthropologists Parker and Gibson, writing together and separately (e.g., Parker and Gibson 1977, 1979; Gibson 1986, n.d.). Although my approach differs in some important ways from Parker and Gibson's, it owes much to theirs, and theirs is the best starting place for understanding the shift point I have outlined.

Extractive foraging can be accomplished with tools or without. Either way it can be described as stereotyped or intelligent, but Parker and Gibson focus on extractive foraging with tools:

> Stereotyped tool use is associated with context-specific foraging on a
> single nonseasonal food source; intelligent tool use is associated with

extractive foraging on a variety of seasonally- and locally-variable encased foods. Intelligent tool use results from trial-and-error and insightful invention of new means to solve a problem. Once a tool-using technique is invented, it may spread through imitation and observational learning in a local population. Intelligent tool use allows species to invent new technology to exploit locally and seasonally variable resources. (Parker and Gibson 1979:371)

For Parker and Gibson, at least two important conclusions follow from a focus on extractive foraging with tools by primates (consult their 1979 article to see how they relate extractive foraging to the evolution of language in hominids). First, "hominid differentiation from the apes was based on a shift from secondary seasonal dependence (as in the case of chimpanzees) to primary year-round dependence on such tool-aided extractive foraging" (1979:371). As I will discuss shortly, the evidence can be interpreted another way as showing a similar level of tool-aided extractive foraging in chimpanzees and early hominids. Parker and Gibson's second conclusion (1979:372) is that food sharing may have arisen as a secondary adaptation for extractive foraging with tools. Because Isaac's view of food sharing as an adaptation for hunting and gathering was then dominant, this suggestion was more radical at the time than it sounds now.

The relevance of a focus on food sharing becomes clear upon reading a passage from Gibson (n.d.):

> The prehistoric ecological transition to extractive foraging on foods that were both difficult to obtain and process would have resulted in mandatory parental provisioning of post weanling children. Abortive attempts by children to open tough nuts, dig deep tubers from the ground and engage in other complex activities would have resulted in need for parental aid. Many parents would have anticipated their children's difficulties in accomplishing these tasks and would have come to their aid as soon as interest was evidenced by the child by pointing, vocalizing, reaching, etc. The probable result would have been that certain vocal or manual gestures would have acquired specific meaning within individual mother-infant pairs.

This scenario suggests a relationship between tool-aided extractive foraging and information donation that goes beyond food sharing itself. Indeed, this speculative reconstruction fits remarkably well with comments made by the primatologist Boesch about information donation among the chimpanzees of Tai, Ivory Coast—a population with heavy seasonal dependence on hard-shelled nuts (see chapter 3). Juveniles at Tai undergo long apprenticeships in learning how to use tools and crack open the hard nuts. Boesch observed some chimpanzee mothers directly guiding their offspring's attempts to carry out tool-aided extractive foraging, and in two cases, he saw maternal teaching of these skills.

Boesch suggests that the complex tool-using skills needed by Tai chimpanzee immatures may be acquired only when true food sharing compensates the immature for the energy devoted to a lengthy apprenticeship. Furthermore, teaching (including the intentional variety implied in Boesch's and Parker and Gibson's formulations, as opposed to the broader definition adopted by Caro and Hauser [1992] and reviewed in chapter 1) might be favored in "situations where the model needs to accelerate the acquisition of a behaviour in an inexperienced individual to prevent any damage to its own reproductive success" (Boesch 1993:173).

Although they need confirmation (see Galef 1992), Boesch's observations add significantly to our understanding of great ape tool use and extractive foraging. Goodall's observations (1973, 1986) also suggest that chimpanzees are the consummate tool-using extractive foragers among primates. Gombe chimpanzees extract termites from mounds and open hard-shelled fruits; they also share food.

With the other great apes, the issue of capacity versus performance reasserts itself. Orangutans, gorillas, and bonobos use tools with dexterity and sophistication in captivity but rarely use them at all in the wild (see reviews by Candland 1987; McGrew 1988, 1992). Orangutans and gorillas solve extractive foraging problems with body size and strength. Parker and Gibson (1977:634) hypothesize that these apes once had the ability to forage extractively with tools but lost it over time when they moved into new habitats in which the appropriate selection pressure was not maintained. Although untestable, this view makes sense of the capacity versus performance disjunction. McGrew (1988:470) may be on target with his comment that "all great apes are smart enough to use tools but they only do so in useful circumstances."

My departure from Parker and Gibson's views can be organized around two points. First, Boesch's chimpanzee data—which were unavailable when Parker and Gibson wrote their original articles—strengthen both Parker and Gibson's proposed relationship between tool-aided extractive foraging and food sharing and my proposed relationship between tool-aided extractive foraging and information donation, but they weaken the suggestion that tool-aided extractive foraging "drove" hominization. Second, many monkeys, some great apes, and, indeed, many nonprimates carry out complicated extractive foraging without tools. Parker and Gibson note this fact but emphasize tool-aided extractive foraging and its relationship to intelligence. Emphasizing that tool-aided extractive foraging need not indicate meaningful cognitive advances is equally important (King 1986).

The cognitive abilities required for some extractive foraging tasks accomplished without tools may be just as complex as those required for extractive foraging with tools. Some birds, for example, including marsh tits, black-capped chickadees, and Clark's nutcrackers, cache food for future recovery, apparently in the absence of sensory cues. Specific criteria used to assess cognition in foraging (see Menzel and Wyers 1981), including the abilities to take into account stimuli that are temporarily absent, to process and react to a large number of variables simultaneously, and to remember and plan ahead, may be applied to the food-recovery behavior of these birds. The resulting analysis (King 1986) suggests that the foraging behavior of birds may be cognitively as complex as some examples of extractive foraging with tools.

In addition, many questions arise from the analysis of birds' foraging behavior. Is acquiring tool-using skills inherently more difficult and time consuming than acquiring other skills needed for complex foraging? More specifically, how do immature birds of these species acquire information socially about foraging, assuming they do so at all? The purported relationship between extractive foraging with tools and food sharing is a separate question, so long as food sharing is not assumed to require particularly well-developed cognitive skills. Even this relationship, however, has not been tested. Is extractive foraging with tools closely correlated with food sharing in primates other than chimpanzees? How often does food sharing occur in primates that do not engage in tool-aided extractive foraging, as it does among callitrichids? These questions await study.

Parker and Gibson's views on extractive foraging are significant for anthropology. Many of their assertions have been strengthened or maintained in the face of new evidence, and all suggest hypotheses for testing. Their work should be read in the original because I have highlighted bits and pieces, inevitably reducing some complex ideas to summaries.

My view is that extractive foraging with tools was unimportant in hominization but highly significant for the evolution of information donation from adults to immatures. To support this assertion, it must be shown that chimpanzees and early hominids depended more on tool-aided extractive foraging than did monkeys, and that chimpanzees and early hominids shared a similar level of tool-aided extractive foraging. More generally, my view assumes that although tool-aided extractive foraging need not correlate with greater cognition, it does correlate with increased information donation. Tool use can be interpreted as behavior that requires guidance and demonstration in ways that other foraging behavior does not—and this requirement is sufficient to select for increased information donation (not the *capacity* for information donation).

Judging from the descriptions by Boesch and McGrew of the dexterity and precision chimpanzees must use in tool-aided extractive foraging, it seems safe to assume that even if tool-using skills are not cognitively more demanding than other tasks, they require a longer period of mastery. When tools are used in foraging, precise "right" and "wrong" solutions exist. In order to solve the problem, specific skills already in use by conspecifics must be mastered, or new tools and processes must be invented.

The first point to address is whether chimpanzees and early hominids depended on tool-aided extractive foraging more than monkeys. According to numerous field studies—at least insofar as negative evidence is reliable— monkeys do not use tools consistently in the wild. Many anecdotes refer to occasional tool use by wild monkeys (Beck 1980; Candland 1987), but hardly ever in the context of extractive foraging. Like most great apes, some monkeys show evidence of far more impressive tool-using skills in captivity than in the wild; the distinction between capacity and performance again confounds issues of evolutionary change and behavioral relationships.

The New World cebus monkey is widely considered the best non-ape tool user (see chapter 3). Indeed, captive cebus monkeys are impressive tool users who solve an unusually wide range of problems with tools, leading Parker and Gibson to classify cebus monkeys with great apes in terms of extractive foraging ability. Parker and Gibson suggest (1977:364) that a certain level of intelligence ("tertiary sensorimotor intelligence" in Piagetian terms) arose "in the common ancestor of cebus monkeys and independently in the common ancestor of the great apes and hominids" as an adaptation for extractive foraging through "complex object manipulation." Visalberghi (1990), who has worked extensively with cebus monkeys, emphasizes, however, that little evidence exists for tool use by wild cebus, and tool behavior by cebus is not qualitatively similar to that known for great apes.

Some debate does exist about the propensity of wild cebus monkeys for tool-use behavior. According to Visalberghi, only one recent, detailed report exists for cebus tool use in the wild (Boinski 1988); it describes a cebus monkey striking a snake with branches. Chevalier-Skolnikoff (1990) observed 31 single acts and 20 bouts (defined as groups of acts that occur in unbroken functional sequences) of tool use during 300 hours of observations on wild cebus monkeys in Costa Rica. Of the 8 types of tool behavior she lists, only 1— probing a hole with a stick—qualifies as extractive foraging. Of the 20 bouts, 17 occurred during aggression, 2 during play, and only 1 during exploration and feeding. Chevalier-Skolnikoff accordingly notes that her data do not support the hypothesis that primate tool use arose as an adaptation for extractive foraging.

Despite the uncertainty about the amount of tool use by wild cebus monkeys, it can be asserted confidently that they do not carry out tool-aided extractive foraging on a regular basis. The same distinction between capacity and performance occurs with cebus monkeys as with so many other primates.

The underlying mechanisms for tool use may be qualitatively different in great apes and cebus monkeys. As Visalberghi (1990:151–52) explains it, "persistent and vigorous trial-and-error attempts using a variety of external objects" are responsible for cebus's success at tool use, whereas chimpanzees show evidence of mental representation. Robust and convincing data support this conclusion (see chapter 3). In sum, despite intriguing examples of occasional tool use by wild monkeys, including cebus, great apes are better at tool-aided extractive foraging than are monkeys.

A similar distinction between great apes and hominids is not supported by the evidence. Our knowledge of early hominid foraging and the Tai chimpanzees' use of tool-aided extractive foraging suggests that australopithecines may not have been significantly better extractive foragers than some great apes. Although this suggestion is speculative, the burden of proof rests with those who support the idea that hominids were better extractive foragers. Many scenarios of early australopithecine foraging focus on adaptation to the savanna and its patchy foods. It will thus be critical to confirm or reject the view that the savanna significantly expanded only well after australopithecines had evolved (see chapter 4). Furthermore, Oldowan tools made by *Homo habilis* show no significant differences from ape tools (Wynn and McGrew 1989). Plausible reconstructions of the early hominid tool kit (Parker and Gibson 1979; Tanner 1981) contain no persuasive evidence to counter the claim that early hominid tools were essentially apelike.

Departing from the classification adopted by Parker and Gibson (1979), I group together apes and early hominids in terms of tool-aided extractive foraging. This classification should not be taken to mean that all apes perform at the level of all early hominids. Rather, it suggests that because some apes, notably some chimpanzees, apparently are as skilled and efficient at (and perhaps nearly as dependent on) tool-aided extractive foraging as were early hominids, there is no compelling reason to suggest that early hominids were better at this behavior than are apes.

The similarity in length of the juvenile period for apes and early hominids fits well with this proposal. Unlike earlier researchers, we now know that apes and australopithecines have roughly equal juvenile periods that are longer than those of other primates (Bromage and Dean 1985; Bromage 1987). The subsequent gradual lengthening of the juvenile period during human evolution must be due to complex factors, but it doubtless allowed more information to be acquired before adulthood and reproduction—and probably required it. When a great deal of information is required to master survival-enhancing technology, then the costs and pressures associated with immatures' acquisition of independent foraging skills should be reduced by donations of both food and information from adults.

Boesch's data and Parker and Gibson's reconstructions of apprenticeships in early hominids bolster the view that tool-aided extractive foraging selects for the donation not only of food but also of information from adults to immatures. The lack of tool-aided extractive foraging by wild monkeys may partially account for the limited information donation they exhibit—in other words, they experience no ecological pressure (at least of the type considered here) toward information donation. A central hypothesis for testing is that the more dependent a particular primate population is on tool-aided extractive foraging, the more information is donated to immatures.

Is the evolution of information donation related to the evolution of cognitive abilities in primates? One possible answer is that important shifts in cognitive ability between monkeys, on the one hand, and chimpanzees and early hominids, on the other, permitted increased information donation. I have already suggested that the differences in extractive foraging abilities between these two groups may not directly relate to cognition. Support for cognitive differences between them comes, however, from the study of other abilities, including attribution. Attribution may be defined as the ability to recognize the mental states of other individuals. Although research into nonhuman primate attribution began over 15 years ago (Premack and Woodruff 1978), only recently has a concentration of talent and energy been devoted to it. Conclusions are still preliminary. As Cheney and Seyfarth (1990:254) phrase it:

> Although most of the data are anecdotal, there is strong suggestive evidence that chimpanzees, if not other apes, recognize that other individuals have beliefs and that their own behavior can affect those beliefs. Unlike monkeys, chimpanzees seem to understand each other's goals and motives. They deceive each other in more ways and in more contexts than monkeys, and they seem better than monkeys at recognizing both their own and other individuals' knowledge and limitations.

Evidence setting chimpanzees apart from monkeys in terms of attributional ability can best be appreciated by understanding four experiments, two each on chimpanzees and macaques. In the pioneering study by Premack and Woodruff (1978), the chimpanzee Sarah was shown videotapes of attempted problem-solving behavior by humans. In one sequence, a human actor tries to reach bananas suspended by a rope from the ceiling (a nice twist on Kohler's [1925] famous experiment with chimpanzees). The video was stopped before the problem was solved, at which point Sarah was shown photographs depicting different potential solutions. Not only was Sarah able to choose the correct photograph for the problem at hand, but she also varied her response according to the identity of the human actor. She chose the correct solution for human actors she liked and incorrect ones for human actors she disliked. Premack and Woodruff (1978:518) suggested that the chimpanzee "imputes at least two states of mind to the human actor, namely, intention or purpose on the one hand, and knowledge or belief on the other"—intention because the chimpanzee assumes the human wants the banana, and knowledge because the chimpanzee assumes that the human knows how to attain the banana.

A recent experiment with chimpanzees focused on the issue of visual perspective taking—the ability to understand how objects and events may appear from another's perspective and that a different visual perspective may cause another individual to have a different state of knowledge from one's own (Povinelli, Nelson, and Boysen 1990). In this study, four chimpanzees (including Sarah) were tested using an apparatus with four pairs of food trays, each covered by an inverted food cup and controllable by handles on one side.

While the chimps watched, human experimenters played the roles of guesser and knower as food was hidden under one cup; the knower hid the food while the guesser was out of the room. When the guesser returned, the knower and guesser pointed to the correct and incorrect locations, respectively (for details see Povinelli, Nelson, and Boysen 1990). The chimpanzee subject then pulled one of the handles on the apparatus. Either the food was revealed and the chimpanzee could obtain it as reward, or the chimpanzee was informed of his or her incorrect choice and shown the correct one. All four chimpanzees consistently chose the correct location significantly more often than the wrong one. Again, the results support the idea that chimpanzees can differentiate among states of knowledge (knowing versus guessing) and can make some inferences about the mental states of others.

The same experiment conducted on rhesus macaques produced a different outcome (Povinelli, Parks, and Novak 1991). The four rhesus subjects showed no obvious discrimination between knower and guesser. These results are consistent with those obtained by Cheney and Seyfarth (1990:231–34) for rhesus and Japanese macaques in another type of experiment. In their study, a juvenile offspring of a high-ranking female was placed in a test area with a subordinate adult female under each of three different conditions: mother (the high-ranking female) visible behind a clear glass barrier (glass condition), mother invisible behind a dark opaque barrier (opaque condition), and mother seated behind a one-way window (mirror condition). In the mirror condition, the mother could be seen by the other two monkeys but could not see them; this condition separated the mother's apparent presence from her knowledge (Cheney and Seyfarth 1990:232). As might be expected from wild studies showing the influence of kin on behavior, juveniles showed more agonistic behavior toward the subordinate female in the glass than in the opaque condition, and subordinate females threatened or supplanted the juveniles more often in the opaque than in the glass condition.

Comparing the glass with the mirror condition was meant to measure the same ability—visual perspective taking—as did the experiments by Povinelli and colleagues. As Cheney and Seyfarth (1990:233) put it, if the subordinate female was capable of distinguishing between her own and the mother's visual perspectives, she might have realized that the mother, though visible, could not see what was happening. In that case her behavior under the mirror condition should have been indistinguishable from that under the opaque condition.

Results from this part of the experiment were mixed. Some aspects of the monkeys' behavior seemed to indicate the ability to distinguish between the mother's presence and her knowledge, whereas others did not. For example, significantly more subordinate females behaved agonistically under the mirror and opaque conditions than under the glass condition, but all subjects spent more time looking at the mother under the mirror and glass conditions than under the opaque. Cheney and Seyfarth conclude that a likely explanation lies in the subjects' skill in monitoring the mother's apparent attentiveness rather than skill at recognizing the mother's mental state (the state of ignorance).

The results of these four experiments, even considered together, are not definitive, but they do strongly suggest that chimpanzees have more highly developed attribution-related abilities than at least some monkeys. A similar conclusion comes from analyzing reports of tactical deceptive behavior in primates (Whiten and Byrne 1988). Deception may be important to consider when discussing social information transfer. When animals can deceive each other behaviorally, a significant cost or risk is introduced to information donation. If an individual uses or depends on information donated by others, it risks being misled by the donor in order for the donor to accrue some advantage. According to kin selection theory, deception should occur at a higher rate among nonrelatives than among relatives. Because the contexts discussed here for social information transfer likely involve kin, I do not treat the costs and risks associated with deception at any length. Nevertheless, theoretical and methodological perspectives that include dishonest information transfer (Dawkins and Krebs 1978; Kaplan 1987; but see Quiatt and Reynolds 1993) should be included in future research on social information transfer.

What is the likely relationship between attribution and information donation? In previous work, only attribution and teaching have been considered together. Opinion is divided between those who propose a direct relationship between them (e.g., Cheney and Seyfarth 1990; Boesch 1991) and those who do not (e.g., Caro and Hauser 1992). Caro and Hauser (1992) clearly show that teaching is possible without a teacher's making inferences about mental states. Other forms of information donation may similarly exist in the absence of attribution. It seems likely, however (and Caro and Hauser do not deny this) that attributional ability aids in information donation, particularly in the guidance or teaching of tasks that are components of complex, multipartite skills such as tool-aided extractive foraging.

Alternative Hypotheses

From a look at the role of apprenticeships by immatures, food sharing, and tool-aided extractive foraging in the evolution of information donation, a central point emerges: the prediction of greater selection pressure for increased information donation in populations that depend on tool-aided extractive foraging. I should reiterate, however, that other, very different conditions might have selected for increased information donation instead of or in addition to the ones proposed here. Any activity that requires sustained attention and long-term practice by immatures—an apprenticeship—might create similar selection pressures. A series of alternative hypotheses and predictions should be considered by primatologists.

Future research might start with the question, With what factors does a high rate of information donation co-occur? Keeping in mind the distinction between ultimate and proximate causes, the underlying goal would be to identify possible selection pressures toward increased information donation. Hypothesis testing could be based on observations made across populations, both within and across species. Ideally, the populations would differ in only one potentially significant factor, although realistically this would be almost impossible.

Some significant factors might include fission-fusion social organization (as in spider monkeys and chimpanzees) versus more cohesive and stable groups (baboons and macaques); more rigid dominance hierarchies (cercopithecines) as compared to weaker or absent dominance hierarchies (some colobines); multiple caretaking of infants (langurs) as opposed to more exclusive mother-infant bonds (baboons); degree of frugivory versus folivory, or degree of dependence on patchy versus evenly distributed foods (spider versus howler monkeys or perhaps western lowland versus mountain gorillas); extractive foraging with tools (chimpanzees) and without tools (gorillas); sharing of nonembedded foods (callitrichids) and of embedded foods (chimpanzees); sharing of embedded foods obtained with tools (chimpanzees) versus embedded foods obtained without tools (orangutans); capacity for attribution (chimpanzees) as opposed to the apparent lack of such a capacity (rhesus macaques); and a well-developed capacity for deception (apes and some monkeys) versus a less well-developed or absent capacity (other monkeys). The challenges in testing for these factors will be, among others, to find appropriate controls and to eliminate alternative hypotheses where possible. Progress can be made both by working with captive populations and by using experimental controls in the field. A similar set of questions could be posed for other aspects of social information transfer, namely, for degree and kind of information acquisition exhibited by immatures.

The paleoanthropological evidence suggests that sometime after *Homo habilis,* most likely during the period of late *Homo erectus,* and again with *Homo sapiens sapiens* at around 40,000 years ago, shifts occurred in information donation that were similar in magnitude to the one separating monkeys from great apes and early hominids. Diachronic approaches should be applied to these shift points as well. Parker and Milbrath (1993), for example, focus on the role of organized planning in human evolution. Their approach is gradualistic, fits with paleoanthropological evidence, including ecological data, and provides a good starting place for modeling change in information donation at later shift points.

I have suggested that behavioral changes in information donation over time can be modeled using diachronic anthropology. The next step for anthropologists is to examine in greater depth the question of change over time using various aspects of social information transfer at various points on the primate continuum. My next step in this book is to address the significance of a focus on information donation for understanding one of the central issues of anthropology, human uniqueness and the role of language in human evolution.

6

INFORMATION DONATION, LANGUAGE, AND HUMAN UNIQUENESS

My central point in this final chapter—which may come as no surprise—is that human communicative behavior, including social information transfer and language, can best be studied along a continuum with that of other primates. Human language can best be understood when compared and contrasted with other forms of information donation that do not rely on language.

This sort of "continuity approach" is in the minority within anthropology (but see Caro and Hauser 1992 and Quiatt and Reynolds 1993 for examples of continuity analysis in other behaviors). Anthropological views of social information transfer and communication fall into three categories, of which the continuity approach is one. In another, some anthropologists (and zoologists, linguists, etc.) posit sharp breaks or discontinuities between the communicative behavior of humans and other animals. The third position recognizes the primate continuum but makes the species-specific language abilities of humans the inevitable standard or starting point for analyses of the evolution of communication and/or the ultimate, superior expression of social information transfer. These last two approaches, which dominate the field, assume or conclude that humans are qualitatively different from other animals by putting language on a higher plane than other forms of information donation.

My intent in this chapter is to consider examples from each of these two perspectives and then to indicate why I believe a different approach is more promising. The continuity approach, one form of which is adopted in this book, holds that quantitative rather than qualitative differences exist in social information transfer across primate species. The continuity approach does not deny the unique properties of human language, but it rejects the view that such properties set human language sharply apart from all other forms of information donation. Furthermore, it allows examination of incremental change in systems of information donation over time.

Although issues surrounding the relationship between language and human uniqueness have a long and rich history, in this chapter I will emphasize recent sources in order to show that the debate continues amply today, even when data about complex nonhuman communication are widely available (i.e., outside technical journals). Textbooks and semipopular books are deemed fair game for evaluation if they are heavily footnoted and trace their conclusions directly to primary works in anthropology. But before embarking on such issues, the relationships of the three approaches to questions of language evolution must be considered.

Evolutionary Analysis of Language

The term *evolution of language* refers variously to the evolution of at least five different processes: vocalizing, speaking, symbolizing, structuring grammar, and developing self-consciousness (Lock 1988). In some of these processes, such as speaking, language is indeed likely to be species-specific to humans (Lieberman 1990). Anthropologists, however, often assume and sometimes conclude that language is species-specific to humans in all these aspects. Their focus then becomes "the evolution of language." My interest encompasses but goes beyond the evolution of language in this sense. I want not only to know how human language skills evolved from those of our common ancestor with great apes but also to model how any behaviors or abilities related to social acquisition or donation of information by primates evolved gradually over time.

If one's interest lies only in the classic evolution-of-language question, is a continuity approach still relevant? Questions about language origins *may,* of course, be subsumed within a larger evolutionary framework focusing on social acquisition and donation of information. I suggest, however, that language *should* be studied without an exclusive focus on species-specific abilities (King 1994). To explain why, I turn to an article by Cartmill (1990) that should be required reading for anyone interested in the origins of language.

Cartmill believes that if language is truly unique to humans, it cannot be explicable in the evolutionary sense. This statement is tremendously significant. Its reasoning is that truly unique behaviors cannot be examined along with other behaviors in search of a common pattern of adaptation, and yet science must proceed by utilizing "an overarching body of theory that governs both the thing itself and its precursors" (Cartmill 1990:188); otherwise, we are left with a mysterious view of language (or of whatever behavior is under consideration).

According to Cartmill, many definitions for human behaviors are constructed explicitly to ensure human uniqueness (see his article for convincing examples). Doing so is unscientific because scientists must "hope to find that the origin of our large brains and language and so on are explained by overarching theoretical regularities that apply to, say, all social animals, or all food-sharing predators, or to whatever categories turn out to have explanatory value and theoretical importance" (Cartmill 1990:189).

Some questions pertinent to studying social information transfer arise from this statement. What categories are used and what theoretical regularities are sought by the proponents of each of the three approaches to the evolution of communication and language? Which of the approaches depend on a species-specific definition—that is, on measuring the behavior of multiple species against a standard taken from human behavior alone? Conversely, which depend on observing, reporting, and comparing the behavior of a variety of species without relying on a human-specific standard? From Cartmill's perspective, can discontinuity theories hope to explain anything about the evolution of language? In turn, can continuity theories explain the novel properties of human communication? Possible answers to these questions emerge from a closer look at the three types of theories.

Discontinuity Views

Writers who argue for discontinuity between the communication of humans and that of other animals typically build their cases in one of two ways. The most straightforward method is to compare and contrast the communication skills of various species and then conclude that human language is by far the most efficient and sophisticated of all communication systems. Language is sometimes defined in such a way as to exclude the communicative skills of other animals.

For Noble and Davidson (1991, 1993), for example, language is the symbolic use of communicative signs to engage in acts of reference. The authors carefully set humans apart from other animals: "Communicative gestures are abundant in the animate world. That they do not amount to language is because the gestures themselves are not recognised by their producers or recipients as the means whereby meanings are communicated. . . . No non-human animals have the capacity to use signs symbolically, at least unaided by humans" (1991:226). The authors explicitly object to any gradualistic approach to "meaning, language, and culture" (1991:232) that might rely on the existence of "prototypes" or precursors.

Throughout their papers, Noble and Davidson rely on rigid dichotomizing of this sort. Indeed, for them, language "transformed" humans (1991:227).

Language permitted not only social identity but also thinking and imagining, so that all these abilities appeared late in human evolution—only in the Upper Paleolithic after 40,000 years ago. The search for language origins must be accomplished by looking for tangible archaeological evidence of signs. To explain the origin of symbols, Noble and Davidson create a scenario in which signs were initially iconic. In their hypothetical example, the accidental freezing of an imitative gesture—mud on a cave wall, in the shape of a zebra—would, in the presence of a dead zebra, allow "the sign itself, and any vocal utterance associated with it . . . to be perceived as a thing that stands for the other thing, as a thing conveying meaning" (1991:245). The authors recognize that this scenario cannot be proven conclusively but claim that it is the kind of scenario needed.

By tying language to the imposition of arbitrary form on the environment via symbol usage, Noble and Davidson dismiss the significance of communication skills in other animals. Their definition of a symbol is narrow, excluding nonhuman behavior altogether. Are they right to say that no other species besides humans routinely uses signs symbolically or imposes arbitrary form on the environment? Might vervet alarm calls or the screams of juvenile macaques be functionally equivalent to symbols because they refer specifically to aspects of the environment? If these vocalizations are not symbols, would Noble and Davidson admit that they are referential and not only emotional? Is there no possible animal precursor to human usage of symbols? If the answer to this last question is no, then a scientific explanation for the appearance of human language is impossible (Cartmill 1990). Moreover, what does it mean that some apes have the capacity to use symbols in enriched environments, when interacting with and guided by humans?

None of these questions appears to be relevant for Noble and Davidson. Except for a brief mention of "tutored" apes, they offer no discussion of alternative types of language skills or language precursors such as referential communication in free-ranging nonhuman primates. Indeed, they seem unaware of or indifferent to data about complex cognition in monkeys and apes, as when they state that "the identification of social identities of any sort before the Upper Paleolithic is problematic" (1991:233). Yet as Quiatt and Reynolds (1993:256) have argued, the ability to "devise categories and communicate them to others" is present in nonhuman primates and probably arose in the arena of kinship. In denying this evidence, Noble and Davidson fall into a trap that plagues many discontinuity theories: assuming that the human form of a particular characteristic is the defining feature of that characteristic.

Similar all-or-nothing statements about language characterize textbooks (e.g., Peoples and Bailey 1991:41, 44, 62) and popular books based on anthropological scholarship (e.g., McCrone 1991). Like thinking and social categories as conceived of by Noble and Davidson, consciousness and self-awareness in humans and other animals may be segregated as rigidly as communication skills. A causal link may be suggested, so that the absence of language traps nonhuman organisms in an unaware, unreflective world. A clear statement to this effect is made in McCrone's *The Ape That Spoke:*

> Before language, the brains of all animals were driven by the demands of the world around them and so were strictly tied to the present moment. Animal brains could only react—even when they were reacting as intelligently as a chimpanzee's brain. But by a stroke of enormous luck, early man managed to evolve language, and once established, language quickly bred new habits of thought that allowed man mentally to break free of his surroundings. Man became an active thinker about life rather than a passive reactor to the events of the world around him. (1991:13)

Yet evidence from primatological field studies (see chapters 2 and 3) clearly refutes any characterization of monkeys and apes as "passive reactors."

A second, rather more complicated position within the discontinuity camp claims that because language is more than just communication, it likely had its origins outside the realm of communication (Bickerton 1990; Burling 1993). The clearest recent example of this perspective is Burling's (1993); he states that language originated "as part of a radically evolving mind"; that is, from cognitive and not communicative arenas. His thesis does not depend on radical discontinuity as does Noble and Davidson's, but claims that nonhuman primate communication is far more similar to most human nonverbal communication (our "gesture-call system") than it is to language:

> [Human nonverbal communication] resembles the communication system of other primates much more closely than it resembles language, and it should be recognized as the primate communication system of the human species. Since our surviving primate communication system remains sharply distinct from language, it is implausible that it could have served as the base from which language evolved. The emergence of language from any earlier primate communication system is equally implausible. (Burling 1993:25)

In supporting this claim, Burling reviews Cheney and Seyfarth's data on referential alarm calling in vervet monkeys and states flatly that "alarm calls, vervet grunts, and smiles of recognition all convey information about the environment, but the information seems hardly significant when set beside the information conveyed by language" (1993:35). "Hardly significant" for whom? How likely is it that information about predators, especially information that specifies the type of approaching predator, would be insignificant for members of a monkey population in which almost half the infants die annually from predation (Cheney and Wrangham 1986:233)? The significance of these calls will remain unknown until we find out how many vervets would die if calls were not uttered at all. The remainder of Burling's analysis is similarly anthropocentric (King 1993a).

Burling's perspective brings us back once more to a central question behind discontinuity theories: Can precursors exist for qualitatively different human abilities? Those who embrace continuity theory would respond by saying that there are no qualitatively different abilities; humans differ only in degree and not in kind from other primates. An intermediate position exists, however, between these two extremes.

Human Language as Starting Place and Standard

Anthropological theories about the evolution of communication cannot simply be separated into discontinuity and continuity camps. Some views belong in a middle ground that asserts no sharp break between humans and nonhuman primates. It notes ungrudgingly the significance of referential abilities in monkeys and apes but holds that even when placed on a continuum, human language is still the implicit standard for complexity and efficiency in communication.

A good example of an intermediate theory comes from Diamond's (1992) *The Third Chimpanzee*. Diamond is knowledgeable about the nonhuman primate data pertaining to emotional versus referential communication, and he discusses them fairly. His approach cannot be lumped with the discontinuity perspective because, for example, he terms vervet referential abilities an "early stage" in the evolution of communication. Diamond also acknowledges that wild chimpanzees and bonobos are not well studied enough to permit adequate description of their communication systems. Diamond goes on to show how human language stands apart from other communication systems. Without language, he says, messages could not be conveyed with great precision. The directive "turn sharp right at the fourth tree and drive the male antelope toward the reddish boulder, where I'll hide to spear it" could not be communicated except through human verbal-auditory channels (Diamond 1992:55). On this point, I agree. Consider, though, how far he takes the argument: "Without language, two protohumans could not brainstorm together about how to devise a better tool, or about what a cave painting might mean. Without language, even one protohuman would have had difficulty thinking out for himself or herself how to devise a better tool" (Diamond 1992:55).

Must brainstorming about how to improve tools be accomplished through language? A scenario can be imagined in which two protohumans, both nonusers of language, work together during problem solving with a tool. They modify the tool in different ways and, through trial and error, assess the effects of these modifications. Because I cannot know whether such a scenario actually occurred in human history, perhaps I am on no firmer ground with my imaginings than Diamond is with his. Nonetheless, I suspect that he has underestimated the power of the nonverbal communication or, at a minimum, of the referential vocal-auditory communication that preceded the appearance of human language (for discussions of how concepts can and do exist independently of language, see Bloch 1991; Kendon 1991).

Diamond's contention that even individuals could not easily modify tools without language is problematic too. Chimpanzees modify tools: they strip leaves off termite wands and they break wooden clubs to make more efficient hammers for nut cracking. Does Diamond restrict the meaning of "devise a better tool" to inventing a new tool type? If so, his view still fails to allow that at some point in their history, chimpanzees must have "invented" the first termite wands or wooden clubs, and done so in the absence of language, at least as Diamond defines it. I see no basis for Diamond's tight linkage of technological abilities and human language. He cites some of the same primatological data as do continuity theorists but interprets them differently. From my perspective, Diamond's type of analysis, by emphasizing human-specific traits as the ultimate standard, impedes a truly evolutionary analysis.

Diamond's book is not an anomaly. Other work that fits my description of scholarship in this intermediate category is that of Lieberman (e.g., 1990, 1991), who explicitly rejects an all-or-nothing dichotomizing of language as absent in animals and present in humans. For Lieberman, the various attributes of human language must be kept separate in analysis because some are phylogenetically older than others. Given that Lieberman recognizes the existence of language before human speech and syntax, why shouldn't his approach be classified as a continuity theory? The key reason is that Lieberman uses certain characteristics of modern human anatomy and speech as the starting point for his analysis and allows these characteristics to furnish the standards by which the traits or abilities of other species—monkeys, apes, and hominids—are measured. The result is a kind of "top down" approach, with modern humans alone at the top.

For studying the evolution of modern human speech, Lieberman's perspective is weakened by its implication—supplied by the constant reference to modern speech as the most rapid and efficient method of all communication systems—that communication before the time of modern humans was inferior, and by its insistence that vocal communication depends on the voluntary control of vocalizations, a control that arose only in humans. In chapter 4, I discussed in some detail how Lieberman seems to misread the primate data as they pertain to communication, particularly voluntary control over vocalizations. Two biological anthropologists (Falk 1992b; Gibson 1994) who are experts in primate neuroanatomy have characterized Lieberman's (1991) book as flawed in this way. My intention here is to add the more subtle point that Lieberman belongs in the middle-ground category between discontinuity and continuity theories because the starting point for his analysis is human anatomy and behavior.

Continuity Approaches

A third type of approach attempts to track and explain incremental changes over time from a different starting point. In continuity approaches, cross-species differences are recognized and explored but are seen primarily as differences of degree. Rarely is the goal of a continuity study simply to compare monkey or ape to human communication and learn from the comparison alone about the origins of human language. Nor is the goal always to search for equivalencies or hierarchies in languagelike properties, such as semanticity, across species. Sometimes, straightforward comparison and contrast does illuminate the modeling of communication by hominids; as explained in chapter 4, the vocal capacities of monkeys or apes—those reflecting referential or voluntary communication—might be used to identify minimal capacities for hominids. But in general, the best continuity approaches go beyond comparison or contrast to correlate behavioral with neuroanatomical changes or otherwise to suggest how and why changes occur.

When gradual changes in communicative and/or cognitive abilities in primates are modeled this way, and especially when possible selection pressures are considered, the results can be powerful. Human language is acknowledged to be different from other communication systems, but the focus remains on understanding what other primates actually do and how behavior changes over time. Instead of undertaking a top-down analysis, the continuity approach works from the bottom up, asking what monkeys and apes *do*, not just whether or not they can do what humans do.

Gibson, whose work on extractive foraging was discussed in chapter 5, has produced scholarship based consistently on a continuity approach (e.g., 1990, 1991, 1994, n.d.). Gibson uses neuroanatomical data to compare and contrast human brains with those of other primates and to ground behavioral shifts across species in measurable neuroanatomical differences. She notes (1990) that the significant differences between the brains of apes and humans are of degree only. Her thesis is that human behaviors often considered to be unique, including language, may not be qualitatively new in primate evolution but may instead represent quantitative increases in functional capacities already present in apes. For Gibson, apes and humans differ most significantly in terms of hierarchically constructed behavior:

> Specifically, expanded brain size [of humans] results in the capacity to hold more perceptual, motor, and conceptual units in mind simultaneously. As a result, humans possess more discrete motor and sensory units than other animals and can combine and recombine these discrete units into more varied and more hierarchically constructed behavioral patterns. Thus, humans possess more finely differentiated oral and manual sensorimotor patterns. (Gibson 1990:98)

As this passage makes clear, Gibson does not deny human uniqueness but views human neural anatomy and behavior as integrated in ways quantitatively different from what we observe in other animals (see Gibson and Ingold 1993).

Gibson goes on to illustrate differences in mental constructional skills by analyzing cross-species abilities in tool use and communication. Human-designed tools are composed of subparts, and in many cases a variety of such tools is used simultaneously or sequentially. Similarly, human speech is composed of vocal sequences that are themselves composed of subcomponents. Tool using and communicative behaviors in apes exhibit a lesser degree of differentiation and variability. Gibson does not define the key difference between primates—change in hierarchically based skills—against a standard of human-specific abilities or properties. She accounts for behavioral shifts by quantitative changes in the brain rather than by the emergence of some qualitatively new trait. In these respects Gibson's scheme differs greatly from Lieberman's and Diamond's, as well as from discontinuity theories.

Hierarchicalization is also an integral part of Greenfield's (1991) continuity theory. Greenfield's use of neuroanatomical data focuses on a region of the brain roughly corresponding to Broca's area. She points out that during a human child's first two years, Broca's area underlies the hierarchical organization of skills in both speech and tool use. After this age, differentiation of neural circuitry occurs, and the two types of behaviors develop separately. In contrast, chimpanzees show identical constraints in speech and tool use throughout life—"the chimpanzee's most advanced combination on the symbolic level matches the structural stage of the chimpanzee's most advanced combination on the tool level" (Greenfield 1991:546).

Taken together, the neuroanatomical and behavioral data suggest to Greenfield that apes do not develop the neural circuitry for hierarchicalization that human children do. Greenfield's work goes beyond child-chimp comparisons to posit an evolutionary "reconstruction in which tool use and manual protolanguage evolved together, both supported by the programming function of the left frontal region associated with Broca's area" (1991:549). It thus accords well with Gibson's theory. Both Greenfield and Gibson see differences in apes and humans as ones of degree, explicable by corresponding quantitative differences in neuroanatomy.

Not every theory about the evolution of language (or social transfer of information) falls neatly into one of my three proposed groups. The categories are meant only to highlight some essential differences in ways to approach the evolution of social information transfer and information donation. Being classifiable as a continuity theory should not be some kind of litmus test for a theory's significance or validity. Parker, who coauthored the extractive foraging papers with Gibson, has also fashioned plausible and stimulating theories (Parker 1985; Parker and Milbrath 1993) that track changes in communication and cognition over time but that are not readily classified within my scheme.

In Parker and Milbrath's (1993) consideration of the evolutionary relationship between language and planning, mentioned in chapter 5, a model is presented for the transition from procedural to declarative planning in human children that could be adapted for other species. Following earlier scholars, Parker and Milbrath use planning theory to define planning based on procedural knowledge as embedded in concrete problem-solving operations, whereas planning based on declarative knowledge involves symbolic representation that allows the planner to anticipate consequences and modify the plan before execution.

After discussing a hierarchy of planning stages and relating them to the skills of human children, Parker and Milbrath compare the abilities of other mammals, including primates, to those of hominids and humans. Even as they write of the large gap between modern humans and great apes in intellectual, linguistic, and planning abilities, they fill this gap with evidence for the planning abilities of hominids. On one hand, then, the article includes a sense of the primate continuum and gradual change over time, based on a good knowledge of primatology and likely selection pressures. On the other hand, the authors conclude that language is critical to declarative planning, and they thus set humans very much apart from other primates. Such a view is based on careful conclusions argued from the ground up, not on assumptions from the top down. As the Parker and Milbrath example underscores, deciding whether a theory advances our understanding of some aspect of the social acquisition or donation of information, not pigeonholing the theory itself, should be the primary goal of the analysis attempted in this chapter.

Language as a Form of Information Donation

The three kinds of theories just reviewed differ in their conceptualization of the relationship between language and other forms of social information donation. Indeed, the discontinuity view sees no precursors for human language, at least not from the arena of vocal communication, and so rejects any consideration of language as part of a larger adaptive complex of communicative behaviors that would include information donation in some nonhuman primates. In the middle-ground perspective, human language is contrasted with other forms of information donation, but because of its unique features, language is thought to be unprecedently complex and efficient.

The continuity approach explains the unique features of human language as quantitative elaborations of earlier communication systems. Skeptical readers might wonder how continuity theorists can possibly deny that human language is a qualitatively different sort of communication. Anyone familiar with the lists of features historically thought to be unique to human language (e.g., displacement, productivity, semanticity, and arbitrariness; Hockett 1960) might ask whether continuity has been found for all such traits. Possible precursors for those features are known for some species (see Boehm 1992), but even when no precursors for specific features of language are known from free-ranging primates, it is still valid to see the human language system as a quantitative elaboration of earlier communication systems.

My reasoning here (and see King 1994), critically important to an understanding of my argument, is similar to that found in two other recent works in zoology and anthropology. Caro and Hauser (1992), in their analysis of teaching in animals, define teaching without reference to human-specific abilities even while recognizing that human teaching might include other, new features compared to teaching in other species. Similarly, Quiatt and Reynolds (1993) adopt a continuity approach to understanding the evolution of the institutionalization of social relationships, that is, human kinship structures and marriage. They do not require the nonhuman form of a behavior to mirror the human form, nor do they say that because marriage is uniquely human, it is without precursors of any type in other animals. Both works allow evolutionary analysis in Cartmill's (1990) sense because they seek regularities and patterns across species. Both are close in spirit to the objective of this book—to show that human language need not be analyzed apart from other forms of information donation just because it contains unique features.

Continuity in more and more features of communication is being discovered between human language and other types of information donation. All forms of information donation, whether vocal or not, involve social interaction that may be intense and prolonged. Yet until recently, studies of animal communication have tended toward a focus on single utterances—the signal as sent by a communicator and received by a second individual—rather than on interactive processes (Snowdon 1988).

Vocal interaction by nonhuman primates is a neglected but promising area of research. Recent data show role differentiation and conversational exchanges, for example, in monkeys. Snowdon (1988) has demonstrated that in uttering contact trills, pygmy marmosets call in individual, patterned sequences much more often than would be expected by chance. Their turn taking is one of three features considered by Symmes and Biben (1988) to be good indicators of conversational vocal exchanges. Squirrel monkeys also give calls—affiliative chuck vocalizations—in ways that indicate conversational ability, leading to the inference that they "are seeking information by questioning and receiving information from answers" (Symmes and Biben 1988:131).

What about the social nature of nonvocal information donation? Consider the social context for some of the behaviors discussed in earlier chapters—for example, maternal guidance of tool-aided extractive foraging in chimpanzees or of choice of social partners in rhesus macaques, and food sharing by adult and immature callitrichids. Assessing the degree to which structured behavioral routines come into play during such adult-immature interactions might be enlightening. Do nonhuman primate adults ever set up predictable routines for immatures, as human adults do in training children in verbal and other skills? Might the teaching of locomotion skills by monkey mothers also be studied from such a perspective?

Mechanisms of information donation, of course, differ across species. Limits to continuity in the form and extent of information donation do exist and require study. Tomasello, Savage-Rumbaugh, and Kruger (n.d.; see also Tomasello, Kruger, and Ratner 1993), for example, suggest that chimpanzee and human adults differ significantly in the types of environments they create for their offspring:

> One reason that wild chimpanzees may not imitatively learn tool use from one another is that, unlike human children, they do not develop in a social environment in which adult conspecifics are constantly encouraging their attention to objects, intentionally teaching them how to use objects as tools, and rewarding them for imitating actions on objects.

Assessing the precise nature of information donation in various species will be helpful in deciding whether there is real merit in analyzing human language as one form among many of social information donation. The view taken here—that discontinuities in certain specific features across various types of information donation do not produce sharply qualitative differences across species—should be scrutinized not just from a variety of theoretical or philosophical stances but also by testing hypotheses on a range of primates.

Conclusion

This book is meant to contribute to a body of anthropological scholarship that rejects discontinuity theory and the use of human-specific skills as the inevitable starting place and standard for evolutionary analysis. Its contribution is organized around four ways of viewing the primatological data.

First, I subscribe to the growing view that infancy is an active period during which primate infants bring considerable skills to creating and maintaining social relationships. My own data, for example, show that free-ranging baboon infants at Amboseli are competent extractors of information about foraging from adults who do not donate information. These data represent one end of a continuum of information transfer within primate foraging and set the stage for describing and explaining evolutionary change along that continuum.

Second, in modeling evolutionary change, I have considered in a new way the significance of the linkages among acquiring hard-to-process food items through tool use, food sharing, and apprenticeship behavior in immatures (see also Parker and Gibson 1979; Boesch 1993; Gibson n.d.*a*). In foraging, primates' dependence on embedded (or otherwise hard-to-process) foods that are acquired with tools and then shared seems to create selection pressures for information donation by adults to immatures. The possibility that such information donation may involve structured routines by adults as well as apprenticeships by active immatures must not be discounted. Much more data need to be collected in ways shaped by hypotheses about information donation. Particularly critical will be finding another primate population (whether of apes or monkeys) that depends on embedded foods to the extent that Tai chimpanzees do, so that appropriate comparisons can be made and these ideas tested more directly.

Third, I view continuity theories as going beyond a focus on infant and adult roles in information acquisition and donation by providing a twist to a classic question. Instead of asking only in what ways humans are unique, it can also be asked how far we can reasonably take the concept of the primate continuum (see King 1993b). A variety of abilities are shared by nonhuman and human primates: expression of social skills during infancy, recognition of complex kinship and dominance relationships, referential rather than purely emotional communication, and voluntary control of some vocalizations. Other tantalizing possibilities for continuity across primate species are only now being investigated, such as those in the area of conversational vocal exchanges.

Fourth, and perhaps most radically, as a direct result of taking the continuity perspective I suggest that the traditional approach to the evolution of human language can be improved by a broader focus on social donation of information. Some anthropologists will, of course, continue to focus exclusively on the properties of human language and on how our human, species-specific adaptations function in communication. Anthropologists must recognize, however, that a focus on human-specific abilities alone cannot lead to *evolutionary* analysis because such analysis requires that we seek common patterns of adaptation within categories of behavior (Cartmill 1990). A focus on social information donation in different species will allow for a program of research that embraces this objective.

These four ways of viewing primatological data are intertwined. They build on previous work by anthropologists and can, in turn, be used to derive hypotheses that, when tested, will add powerfully to our understanding of the evolution of the social acquisition and donation of information and of the behavior of primates, both nonhuman and human.

References

Altmann, J.
  1974   Observational study of behavior: Sampling methods. Behaviour 49:213–66.
  1980   Baboon Mothers and Infants. Cambridge: Harvard University Press.
Altmann, S.
  1967   The structure of primate social communication. *In* Social Communication among Primates. S. Altmann, ed., pp. 325–62. Chicago: University of Chicago Press.
Altmann, S., and J. Altmann
  1970   Baboon Ecology: African Field Research. Chicago: University of Chicago Press.
Andersen, D. C.
  1987   Below-ground herbivory in natural communities: A review emphasizing fossorial animals. Quarterly Review of Biology 63:261–86.
Arensburg, B., L. A. Schepartz, A. M. Tillier, B. Vandermeersch, and Y. Rak
  1990   A reappraisal of the anatomical basis for speech in Middle Palaeolithic hominids. American Journal of Physical Anthropology 83:137–46.
Baldwin, J. D.
  1986   Behavior in infancy: Exploration and play. *In* Comparative Primate Biology, vol. 2, pt. A: Behavior, Conservation and Ecology. G. Mitchell and J. Erwin, eds., pp. 295–326. New York: Alan R. Liss.
Bard, K. A.
  1990   "Social tool use" by free-ranging orangutans: A Piagetian and developmental perspective on the manipulation of an animate object. *In* "Language" and Intelligence in Monkeys and Apes. S. T. Parker and K. Gibson, eds., pp. 356–78. Cambridge: Cambridge University Press.
Beck, B. B.
  1980   Animal Tool Behavior. New York: Garland Press.
  1982   Chimpocentrism: Bias in cognitive ethology. Journal of Human Evolution 11:3–17.
Berman, C. M.
  1982a   The ontogeny of social relationships with group companions among free-ranging infant rhesus monkeys, I: Social networks and differentiation. Animal Behaviour 30:149–62.
  1982b   The ontogeny of social relationships with group companions among free-ranging infant rhesus monkeys, II: Differentiation and attractiveness. Animal Behaviour 30:163–70.
Bernstein, I. S.
  1988   Metaphor, cognitive belief, and science. Behavioral and Brain Sciences 11(2):247–48.
  1991   The correlation between kinship and behaviour in non-human primates. *In* Kin Recognition. P. G. Hepper, ed., pp. 6–29. Cambridge: Cambridge University Press.
Bickerton, D.
  1990   Language and Species. Chicago: University of Chicago Press.
Binford, L. R.
  1989   Debating Archaeology. New York: Academic Press.
Bloch, M.
  1991   Language, anthropology and cognitive science. Man 26:183–98.
Boehm, C.
  1989   Methods for isolating chimpanzee vocal communication. *In* Understanding Chimpan-

zees. P. G. Heltne and L. A. Marquardt, eds., pp. 38–59. Cambridge: Harvard University Press.

1992   Vocal communication of *Pan troglodytes:* "Triangulating" to the origin of spoken language. *In* Language Origin: A Multidisciplinary Approach. J. Wind, ed., pp. 323–50. Boston: Kluwer Academic.

Boesch, C.
1991   Teaching among chimpanzees. Animal Behaviour 41:530–32.
1993   Aspects of transmission of tool-use in wild chimpanzees. *In* Tools, Language and Cognition in Human Evolution. K. Gibson and T. Ingold, eds., pp. 171–83. Cambridge: Cambridge University Press.

Boesch, C., and H. Boesch
1981   Sex differences in the use of natural hammers by wild chimpanzees: A preliminary report. Journal of Human Evolution 10:585–93.
1983   Optimisation of nut-cracking with natural hammers by wild chimpanzees. Behaviour 83(3–4):265–86.
1984   Mental map in wild chimpanzees: An analysis of hammer transports for nutcracking. Primates 25(2):160–70.
1989   Hunting behavior of wild chimpanzees in the Tai National Park. American Journal of Physical Anthropology 78:547–73.
1990   Tool use and tool making in wild chimpanzees. Folia Primatologica 54:86–99.

Boinski, S.
1988   Use of a club by a wild white-faced capuchin (*Cebus capucinus*) to attack a venomous snake (*Bothrops asper*). American Journal of Primatology 14:177–79.

Boinski, S., and D. M. Fragaszy
1989   The ontogeny of foraging in squirrel monkeys, *Saimiri oerstedi.* Animal Behaviour 37:415–28.

Bonner, J. T.
1980   The Evolution of Culture in Animals. Princeton: Princeton University Press.

Boyd, R., and P. J. Richerson
1985   Culture and the Evolutionary Process. Chicago: University of Chicago Press.

Brazelton, T. B.
1979   Evidence of communication during neonatal behavioral assessment. *In* Before Speech: The Beginning of Interpersonal Communication. M. B. Bullowa, ed. Cambridge: Cambridge University Press.

Bromage, T. G.
1987   The biological and chronological maturation of early hominids. Journal of Human Evolution 16:257–72.

Bromage, T. G., and M. C. Dean
1985   Re-evaluation of the age at death of immature fossil hominids. Nature 317:525–27.

Brown, K., and D. S. Mack
1978   Food sharing among captive *Leontopithecus rosalia.* Folia Primatologica 29:288–90.

Bruner, J.
1983   Child's Talk. Oxford: Oxford University Press.

Burling, R.
1993   Primate calls, human language and nonverbal communication. Current Anthropology 34(1):25–53.

Busse, C. D.
1978   Do chimpanzees hunt cooperatively? American Naturalist 112:767–70.

Butynski, T. M.
1982   Vertebrate predation by primates: A review of hunting patterns and prey. Journal of Human Evolution 11:421–30.

Byrne, R. W., and A. Whiten
1985   Tactical deception of familiar individuals in baboons (*Papio ursinus*). Animal Behaviour 33(2):669–73.

Cambefort, J. P.
1981   A comparative study of culturally transmitted patterns of feeding habits in the chacma baboon (*Papio ursinus*) and the vervet monkey (*Cercopithecus aethiops*). Folia Primatologica 36:243–63.

Campbell, B. G.
1992   Humankind Emerging. 6th ed. New York: HarperCollins.
Candland, D. K.
1987   Tool use. *In* Comparative Primate Biology, vol. 2, pt. B: Behavior, Cognition and Motivation. G. Mitchell and J. Erwin, eds., pp. 85–103. New York: Alan R. Liss.
Cant, J. G. H., and L. A. Temerin
1984   A conceptual approach to foraging adaptations in primates. *In* Adaptations for Foraging in Nonhuman Primates. P. S. Rodman and J. G. H. Cant, eds., pp. 304–42. New York: Columbia University Press.
Caro, T. M., and M. D. Hauser
1992   Is there teaching in nonhuman animals? Quarterly Review of Biology 67(2):151–74.
Cartmill, M.
1990   Human uniqueness and theoretical content in paleoanthropology. International Journal of Primatology 11(3):173–92.
Chase, P. G., and H. L. Dibble
1987   Middle Paleolithic symbolism: A review of current evidence and interpretations. Journal of Anthropological Archaeology 10:193–214.
Cheney, D. L.
1977   The acquisition of rank and the development of reciprocal alliances among free-ranging immature baboons. Behavioral Ecology and Sociobiology 2:303–18.
Cheney, D. L., and R. M. Seyfarth
1982   How vervet monkeys perceive their grunts: Field playback experiments. Animal Behaviour 30:739–51.
1990   How Monkeys See the World. Chicago: University of Chicago Press.
Cheney, D. L., and R. W. Wrangham
1986   Predation. *In* Primate Societies. B. B. Smuts, D. L. Cheney, R. M. Seyfarth, R. W. Wrangham, and T. T. Struhsaker, eds., pp. 227–39. Chicago: University of Chicago Press.
Cheney, D. L., R. M. Seyfarth, and B. B. Smuts
1986   Social relationships and social cognition in nonhuman primates. Science 234:1361–66.
Chevalier-Skolnikoff, S.
1990   Tool use by wild cebus monkeys at Santa Rosa National Park, Costa Rica. Primates 31(3):375–83.
Chism, J.
1991   Ontogeny of behavior in humans and nonhuman primates: The search for common ground. *In* Understanding Behavior: What Primate Studies Tell Us about Human Behavior. J. D. Loy and C. B. Peters, eds., pp. 99–120. New York: Oxford University Press.
Clutton-Brock, T. H., and P. H. Harvey
1980   Primates, brains and ecology. Journal of Zoology 190:309–23.
Conkey, M. W.
1978   Style and information in cultural evolution: Toward a predictive model for the Paleolithic. *In* Social Archaeology. C. L. Redman, M. J. Berman, E. V. Curtin, W. T. Langhorne, N. M. Versaggi, and J. C. Wanser, eds., pp. 61–85. New York: Academic Press.
1987   New approaches in the search for meaning? A review of research in "Paleolithic Art." Journal of Field Archaeology 4:413–30.
Conkey, M. W., and C. A. Hastorf
1990   The uses of style in archaeology. Cambridge: Cambridge University Press.
Conroy, G. C.
1990   Primate Evolution. New York: W. W. Norton.
Cook, M., S. Mineka, B. Wolkenstein, and K. Laitsch
1985   Observational conditioning of snake fear in unrelated rhesus monkeys. Journal of Abnormal Psychology 94(4):591–610.
1989   Observational conditioning of fear to fear-relevant versus fear-irrelevant stimuli in rhesus monkeys. Journal of Abnormal Psychology 98(4):448–59.
Davidson, I.
1989   Freedom of information: Aspects of art and society in western Europe during the last Ice Age. *In* Animals into Art. H. Morphy, ed., pp. 440–56. London: Unwin Hyman.
Dawkins, R., and J. R. Krebs
1978   Animal signals: Information or manipulation? *In* Behavioral Ecology, an Evolutionary

Approach. J. R. Krebs and N. B. Davies, eds., pp. 282–309. Oxford: Blackwell Scientific Publications.

Dennett, D. C.
1987   The Intentional Stance. Cambridge: MIT/Bradford Books.

Deputte, B.
1982   Duetting in male and female songs of the white-cheeked gibbon (*Hylobates concolor leucogenys*). *In* Primate Communication. C. T. Snowdon, C. H. Brown, and M. Petersen, eds. Cambridge: Cambridge University Press.

Dettwyler, K. A.
1989   Styles of infant feeding: Parental/caretaker control of food consumption in young children. American Anthropologist 91:696–703.
1991   Can paleopathology provide evidence for "compassion"? American Journal of Physical Anthropology 84:375–84.

DeVore, I.
1990   Introduction: Current studies on primate socioecology and evolution. International Journal of Primatology 11(1):1–5.

DeVore, I., and S. L. Washburn.
1963   Baboon ecology and human evolution. *In* African Ecology and Human Evolution. F. C. Howell and F. Bourliere, eds., pp. 335–67. New York: Wenner-Gren Foundation.

de Waal, F. B. M.
1990   Do rhesus mothers suggest friends to their offspring? Primates 31(4):597–600.

Diamond, J.
1992   The Third Chimpanzee: The Evolution and Future of the Human Animal. New York: HarperCollins.

Dibble, H. L.
1987   The interpretation of Middle Paleolithic scraper morphology. American Antiquity 52:109–117.
1989   The implications of stone tool types for the presence of language during the Lower and Middle Palaeolithic. *In* The Human Revolution: Behavioural and Biological Perspectives on the Origins of Modern Humans. P. Mellars and C. Stringer, eds., pp. 415–31. Princeton: Princeton University Press.

Dittus, W. P. J.
1984   Toque macaque food calls: Semantic communication concerning food distribution in the environment. Animal Behaviour 32:470–77.

Dolhinow, P.
1991   Tactics of primate immaturity. *In* Man and Beast Revisited. M. H. Robinson and L. Tiger, eds., pp. 139–57. Washington, D.C.: Smithsonian Institution Press.

Dolhinow, P., and M. DeMay
1982   Adoption: The importance of infant choice. Journal of Human Evolution 11:391–420.

Dolhinow, P., and G. Murphy
1982   Langur monkey (*Presbytis entellus*) development: The first three months of life. Folia Primatologica 39:305–31.

Fairbanks, L. A.
1988   Vervet monkey grandmothers: Interactions with infant grandoffspring. International Journal of Primatology 90(5):425–41.

Falk, D. A.
1992a   Braindance. New York: Henry Holt.
1992b   Review of Uniquely Human: The Evolution of Speech, Thought and Selfless Behavior, by Philip Lieberman. International Journal of Primatology 13(2):217–20.

Feinman, S.
1985   Emotional expression, social referencing, and preparedness for learning in infancy— Mother knows best, but sometimes I know better. *In* The Development of Expressive Behavior. G. Zivin, ed., pp. 291–318. New York: Academic.

Feistner, A., and W. C. McGrew
1989   Food-sharing in primates: A critical review. *In* Perspectives in Primate Biology, vol. 3. P. K. Seth and S. Seth, eds., pp. 21–36. New Delhi: Today and Tomorrow's Printers and Publishers.

Ferrari, S. F.
1987   Food transfer in a wild marmoset group. Folia Primatologica 48:203–206.

Foley, R. A.
1987   Another Unique Species. New York: John Wiley and Sons.
1989   The search for early man. Archaeology, Jan./Feb., pp. 27–32.
1991   How useful is the concept of culture? In The Origins of Human Behaviour. R. A. Foley, ed., pp. 25–38. London: Unwin Hyman.

Fossey, D.
1979   Development of the mountain gorilla (Gorilla gorilla beringei): The first thirty-six months. In The Great Apes. D. A. Hamburg and E. R. McCown, eds., pp. 138–84. Menlo Park, CA: Benjamin/Cummings.

Fragaszy, D. M., and E. Visalberghi
1990   Social processes affecting the appearance of innovative behaviors in capuchin monkeys. Folia Primatologica 54:155–65.

Galef, B. G.
1988   Imitation in animals: History, definition and interpretation of data from the psychological laboratory. In Social Learning: Psychological and Biological Perspectives. T. Zentall and B. G. Galef, eds., pp. 3–28. Hillsdale, NJ: Erlbaum.
1991   Tradition in animals: Field observations and laboratory analyses. In Interpretation and Explanation in the Study of Animal Behavior. M. Bekoff and D. Jamieson, eds., pp. 74–95. Boulder: Westview Press.
1992   The question of animal culture. Human Nature 3(2):157–78.

Gamble, C.
1983   Culture and society in the Upper Paleolithic of Europe. In Hunter-Gatherer Economy in Prehistory: A European Perspective. G. Bailey, ed., pp. 201–11. New York: Cambridge University Press.

Gero, J. M.
1989   Assessing social information in material objects: How well do lithics measure up? In Time, Energy, and Stone Tools. R. Torrence, ed., pp. 92–105. Cambridge: Cambridge University Press.

Ghiglieri, M. P.
1984   The Chimpanzees of Kibale Forest: A Field Study of Ecology and Social Structure. New York: Columbia University Press.

Gibson, K. R.
1986   Cognition, brain size and extraction of embedded foods. In Primate Ontogeny and Social Behaviour. J. C. Else and P. C. Lee, eds., pp. 93–105. Cambridge: Cambridge University Press.
1990   New perspectives in instincts and intelligence: Brain size and the emergence of hierarchical mental constructional skills. In "Language" and Intelligence in Monkeys and Apes. S. T. Parker and K. R. Gibson, eds., pp. 97–128. Cambridge: Cambridge University Press.
1991   Tools, language and intelligence: Evolutionary implications. Man (n.s.) 26:255–64.
1994   Continuity theories of human language origins versus the Lieberman model. Language and Communication 14(1):97–114.
n.d.   The ontogeny and evolution of the brain, cognition and language. In Handbook of Symbolic Intelligence. A. Lock and C. Peters, eds. Oxford University Press. In press.

Gibson, K. R., and T. Ingold
1993   Tools, Language, and Cognition in Human Evolution. Cambridge: Cambridge University Press.

Glander, K. E.
1982   The impact of plant secondary compounds on primate feeding behavior. Yearbook of Physical Anthropology 25:1–18.

Goldizen, A. W.
1986   Tamarins and marmosets: Communal care of offspring. In Primate Societies. B. B. Smuts, D. L. Cheney, R. M. Seyfarth, R. W. Wrangham, and T. T. Struhsaker, eds., pp. 34–43. Chicago: University of Chicago Press.

Goodall, J.
  1973   Cultural elements in the chimpanzee community. *In* Precultural Primate Behavior. E. W. Menzel, ed., pp. 144–84. Basel: S. Karger.
  1986   The Chimpanzees of Gombe: Patterns of Behavior. Cambridge, MA: Belknap Press.
  1990   Through a Window: My Thirty Years with the Chimpanzees of Gombe. Boston: Houghton Mifflin.

Gould, J. L.
  1986   The biology of learning. Annual Review of Psychology 37:163–92.

Gouzoules, H., and S. Gouzoules
  1989   Design features and developmental modification of pigtail macaque, *Macaca nemestrina*, agonistic screams. Animal Behaviour 37:383–401.

Gouzoules, S., and H. Gouzoules
  1986   Kinship. *In* Primate Societies. B. B. Smuts, D. L. Cheney, R. M. Seyfarth, R. W. Wrangham, and T. T. Struhsaker, eds., pp. 299–305. Chicago: University of Chicago Press.

Gouzoules, S., H. Gouzoules, and P. Marler
  1984   Rhesus monkey (*Macaca mulatta*) screams: Representational signalling in the recruitment of agonistic aid. Animal Behaviour 32:182–93.

Greenfield, P. M.
  1991   Language, tools and the brain: The ontogeny and phylogeny of hierarchically organized sequential behavior. Behavioral and Brain Sciences 14:531–95.

Greenfield, P. M., and E. S. Savage-Rumbaugh
  1990   Grammatical combination in *Pan paniscus:* Processes of learning and invention in the evolution and development of a language. *In* "Language" and Intelligence in Monkeys and Apes. S. T. Parker and K. R. Gibson, eds., pp. 540–78. Cambridge: Cambridge University Press.

Hall, K. R. L.
  1963   Tool using performance as indicators of behavioral adaptability. *In* Primate Behavior: Studies in Adaptation and Variability. P. C. Jay, ed., pp. 131–48. New York: Holt, Rinehart and Winston.

Halverson, J.
  1987   Art for art's sake in the Paleolithic. Current Anthropology 28:63–89.

Hannah, A., and W. McGrew
  1987   Chimpanzees using stones to crack open oil palm nuts in Liberia. Primates 28:31–46.

Harcourt, A. H.
  1992   Coalitions and alliances: Are primates more complex than non-primates? *In* Coalitions and Alliances in Humans and Other Animals. A. H. Harcourt and F. de Waal, eds., pp. 444–71. New York: Oxford University Press.

Harding, R. S. O.
  1991   Three decades of anthropological primatology. Reviews in Anthropology 18:235–45.

Harkness, S., and C. M. Super
  1985   The cultural context of gender segregation in children's peer groups. Child Development 56:219–24.

Hatley, T., and S. Kappelman
  1980   Bears, pigs, and Plio-Pleistocene hominids: A case for the exploitation of belowground food resources. Human Ecology 8:371–87.

Hauser, M. D.
  1988   Invention and social transmission: New data from wild vervet monkeys. *In* Machiavellian Intelligence. R. W. Byrne and A. Whiten, eds., pp. 327–43. Oxford: Clarendon Press.

Hauser, M. D., and P. Marler
  1993a   Food-associated calls in rhesus macaques (*Macaca mulatta*). I: Socioecological factors. Behavioral Ecology 4:194–205.
  1993b   Food-associated calls in rhesus macaques (*Macaca mulatta*). II: Costs and benefits of call production and suppression. Behavioral Ecology 4:206–12.

Hausfater, G.
  1975   Dominance and reproduction in baboons (*Papio cynocephalus*). Contributions to Primatology 7. Basel: S. Karger.

Hewlett, B. S.
    1991a   Intimate Fathers: The Nature and Context of Aka Pygmy Paternal Infant Care. Ann Arbor: University of Michigan Press.
    1991b   Demography and childcare in preindustrial societies. Journal of Anthropological Research 47(1):1–37.
Hinde, R. A., and M. J. A. Simpson
    1975   Qualities of mother-infant relationships in monkeys. *In* Parent-Infant Interaction. Ciba Foundation Symposium 33. Amsterdam: Elsevier.
Hiraiwa-Hasegawa, M.
    1990a   Role of food sharing between mother and infant in the ontogeny of feeding behavior. *In* The Chimpanzees of the Mahale Mountains: Sexual and Life History Strategies. T. Nishida, ed., pp. 267–75. Tokyo: University of Tokyo Press.
    1990b   A note on the ontogeny of feeding. *In* The Chimpanzees of the Mahale Mountains: Sexual and Life History Strategies. T. Nishida, ed., pp. 277–83. Tokyo: University of Tokyo Press.
Hockett, C. F.
    1960   Logical considerations in the study of animal communication. *In* Animal Sounds and Communication. W. E. Lanyon and W. N. Tavolga, eds., pp. 392–430. Washington: American Institute of Biological Science.
Horr, D. A.
    1977   Orang-utan maturation: Growing up in a female world. *In* Primate Bio-social Development: Biological, Social and Ecological Determinants. S. Chevalier-Skolnikoff and F. E. Poirer, eds., pp. 289–321. New York: Garland Press.
Isaac, G.
    1978   The food-sharing behavior of protohuman hominids. Scientific American 238(4):90–108.
    1980   Casting the net wide: A review of archaeological evidence for early hominid land-use and ecological relations. *In* Current Argument on Early Man. L. Koniggson, ed., pp. 226–51. Oxford: Pergamon Press.
    1986   Foundation stones: Early artifacts as indicators of activities and abilities. *In* Stone Age Prehistory. G. N. Bailey and P. Callow, eds., pp. 221–41. Cambridge: Cambridge University Press.
Izawa, K., and A. Mizuno
    1977   Palm-fruit cracking behavior of wild black-capped capuchin (*Cebus apella*). Primates 18(4):773–97.
Jay, P.
    1963   Mother-infant relations in langurs. *In* Maternal Behaviour in Mammals. H. L. Reingold, ed., pp. 282–309. New York: John Wiley and Sons.
Jochim, M. A.
    1983   Palaeolithic cave art in ecological perspective. *In* Hunter-Gatherer Economy in Prehistory: A European Perspective. G. Bailey, ed., pp. 212–19. New York: Cambridge University Press.
Johnson, R. L.
    1986   Mother-infant contact and maternal maintenance activities among free-ranging rhesus monkeys. Primates 27:191–203.
Jolly, C. J., and F. Plog
    1986   Physical Anthropology and Archaeology. 4th ed. New York: Alfred Knopf.
Kano, T.
    1992   The Last Ape: Pygmy Chimpanzee Behavior and Ecology. Stanford, CA: Stanford University Press.
Kaplan, H.
    1987   Human communication and contemporary evolutionary theory. Research on Language and Social Interaction 20:79–139.
Kawamura, S.
    1959   The process of sub-culture propagation among Japanese macaques. Primates 2:43–60.
Kendon, A.
    1991   Some considerations for a theory of language origins. Man 26:199–221.

King, B. J.
  1986   Extractive foraging and the evolution of primate intelligence. Human Evolution
          1(4):361–72.
  1989   Social information transfer and foraging in yellow baboon (*Papio cynocephalus*) in-
          fants. Ph.D. dissertation, University of Oklahoma. Ann Arbor: University Microfilms.
  1991   Social information transfer in monkeys, apes, and hominids. Yearbook of Physical
          Anthropology 34:97–115.
  1993a   Comment. Current Anthropology 34(1):40–41.
  1993b   The primate behavioral continuum: What are its limits? Behavioral and Brain Sciences
          16(3):527–28.
  1994   Evolutionism, essentialism, and an evolutionary perspective on language: Moving be-
          yond a human standard. Language and Communication 14(1):1–13.
  n.d.   Primate infants as skilled information gatherers. Pre- and Perinatal Psychology Journal
          8(4). In press.
Kinzey, W.
  1987   The Evolution of Human Behavior: Primate Models. New York: State University of New
          York Press.
Kinzey, W. G., and M. A. Norconk
  1990   Hardness as a basis of fruit choice in two sympatric primates. American Journal of
          Physical Anthropology 81:5–15.
Kitahara-Frisch, J.
  1993   The origin of secondary tools. *In* The Use of Tools by Human and Non-human Primates.
          A. Berthelet and J. Chavaillon, eds., pp. 239–46. Oxford: Clarendon Press.
Kohler, W.
  1925   The Mentality of Apes. 2d ed., 1959. New York: Viking.
Kroeber, A. L., and C. Kluckhohn
  1952   Culture: A critical review of concepts and definitions. Papers of the Peabody Museum
          of American Archeology and Ethnology 47:41–72.
Kummer, H.
  1968   Social Organization of Hamadryas Baboons: A Field Study. Basel: S. Karger.
  1971   Primate Societies. Chicago: Aldine.
  1982   Social knowledge in free-ranging primates. *In* Animal Mind–Human Mind. D. Griffin,
          ed., pp. 113–30. Berlin: Springer-Verlag.
Kurland, J. A., and S. J. Beckerman
  1985   Optimal foraging and hominid evolution: Labor and reciprocity. American Anthropolo-
          gist 87:73–93.
Lancaster, J. B.
  n.d.   Parental investment and the evolution of the juvenile phase of the human life course.
          In The Origins of Humanness. A. Brooks, ed. Washington, DC: Smithsonian Institution
          Press. In press.
Lancaster, J. B., and C. S. Lancaster
  1983   Parental investment: The hominid adaptation. *In* How Humans Adapt: A Biocultural
          Odyssey. D. J. Ortner, ed., pp. 33–56. Washington, D.C.: Smithsonian Institution Press.
  1987   The watershed: Change in parental-investment and family-formation strategies in the
          course of human evolution. *In* Parenting Across the Life Span: Biosocial Dimensions.
          J. B. Lancaster, J. Altmann, A. S. Rossi, and L. R. Sherrod, eds., pp. 187–205. Hawthorne,
          NY: Aldine de Gruyter.
Le Gros Clark, W.
  1959   The Antecedents of Man. Edinburgh: Edinburgh University Press.
Lieberman, P.
  1990   The evolution of human language. Seminars in Speech and Language 11(2):63–76.
  1991   Uniquely Human: The Evolution of Speech, Thought and Selfless Behavior. Cambridge:
          Harvard University Press.
Lock, A.
  1988   Implication and the evolution of language. *In* The Genesis of Language: A Different
          Judgment of Evidence. M. E. Landsberg, ed., pp. 89–100. Berlin: Mouton de Gruyter.
Lovejoy, C. O.
  1988   The evolution of human walking. Scientific American 259:118–25.

McCrone, J.
1991   The Ape That Spoke: Language and the Evolution of the Human Mind. New York: William Morrow.
McGrew, W. C.
1975   Patterns of plant food sharing by wild chimpanzees. *In* Contemporary Primatology: Proceedings of the Fifth Congress of the International Primatological Society. M. Kawai, S. Kondo, and A. Ehara, eds., pp. 304–309. Basel: S. Karger.
1977   Socialization and object manipulation of wild chimpanzees. *In* Primate Biosocial Development. S. Chevalier-Skolnikoff and F. Poirer, eds., pp. 261–88. New York: Garland Press.
1979   Evolutionary implications of sex differences in chimpanzee predation and tool use. *In* The Great Apes. D. A. Hamburg and E. R. McCown, eds., pp. 440–63. Menlo Park, CA: Benjamin/Cummings.
1988   Why is ape tool use so confusing? *In* Comparative Socioecology. R. A. Foley and V. Standen, eds., pp. 457–72. Oxford: Blackwell Scientific.
1991   Chimpanzee material culture: What are its limits and why? *In* The Origins of Human Behaviour. R. A. Foley, ed., pp. 13–24. London: Unwin Hyman.
1992   Chimpanzee Material Culture. Cambridge: Cambridge University Press.
McKenna, J. J.
1981   Primate infant caregiving behavior. *In* Parental Care in Mammals. D. J. Gubernik and P. H. Klopfer, eds., pp. 389–416. New York: Plenum Press.
Macphail, E. M.
1987   The comparative psychology of intelligence. Behavioral and Brain Sciences 10:645–95.
Markl, H.
1985   Manipulation, modulation, information, cognition: Some of the riddles of communication. *In* Experimental Behavioral Ecology and Sociobiology. B. Holldobler and M. Lindauer, eds., pp. 163–94. Stuttgart: Gustaf Fischer Verlag; Sunderland, MA: Sinauer Associates.
Marler, P.
1985   Representational vocal signals in primates. *In* Experimental Behavioral Ecology and Sociobiology. B. Holldobler and M. Lindauer, eds., pp. 211–21. Stuttgart: Gustav Fischer Verlag; Sunderland, MA: Sinauer Associates.
Marshack, A.
1989   Evolution of the human capacity: The symbolic evidence. Yearbook of Physical Anthropology 32:1–34.
Mason, W.
1979   Ontogeny of social behavior. *In* Handbook of Behavioral Neurobiology, vol. 3: Social Behavior and Communication. P. Marler and J. Vandenberg, eds., pp. 1–28. New York: Plenum Press.
Mellars, P.
1991   Cognitive changes and the emergence of modern humans in Europe. Cambridge Archaeological Journal 1(1):63–76.
Mellars, P., and C. Stringer
1989   The Human Revolution: Behavioural and Biological Perspectives on the Origins of Modern Humans. Princeton: Princeton University Press.
Meltzoff, A. N.
1988   Imitation, objects, tools and the rudiments of language in human ontogeny. Human Evolution 3:45–64.
Menzel, E. W., and E. J. Wyers
1981   Cognitive aspects of foraging behavior. *In* Foraging Behavior. A. C. Kamil and T. D. Sargent, eds. New York: Garland STPM Press.
Milton, K.
1979   Factors influencing leaf choice by howler monkeys: A test of some hypotheses of food selection by generalist herbivores. American Naturalist 114:362–78.
1981   Distribution patterns of tropical plant foods as an evolutionary stimulus to primate mental development. American Anthropologist 83:534–48.
1988   Foraging behaviour and the evolution of primate intelligence. *In* Machiavellian Intelligence. R. Byrne and A. Whiten, eds., pp. 285–305. Oxford: Clarendon Press.

1993   Diet and social organization of a free-ranging spider monkey population: The develop-
        ment of speices-typical behavior in the absence of adults. *In* Juvenile Primates. M. E.
        Pereira and L. A. Fairbanks, eds., pp. 173–81. New York: Oxford University Press.

Mineka, S., M. Davidson, M. Cook, and R. Keir
1984   Observational conditioning of snake fear in rhesus monkeys. Journal of Abnormal Psy-
        chology 93:355–72.

Mithen, S. J.
1988   Looking and learning: Upper Paleolithic art and information gathering. World Archae-
        ology 19:297–327.

Mueller-Wille, C. S., and D. B. Dickson
1991   An examination of some models of late Pleistocene society in southwestern Europe.
        In Perspectives on the Past. G. A. Clark, ed., pp. 25–55. Philadelphia: University of
        Pennsylvania Press.

Nicholson, N.
1982   Weaning and the development of independence in olive baboons. Ph.D. dissertation,
        Harvard University.

Nishida, T.
1986   Local traditions and cultural transmission. *In* Primate Societies. B. B. Smuts, D. L.
        Cheney, R. M. Seyfarth, R. W. Wrangham, and T. T. Struhsaker, eds., pp. 462–74. Chicago:
        University of Chicago Press.

Nishida, T., and S. Uehara
1983   Natural diet of chimpanzees (*Pan troglodytes schweinfurthii*): Long-term record from
        the Mahale Mountains, Tanzania. African Studies Monographs 3:109–30.

Nishida, T., R. W. Wrangham, J. Goodall, and S. Uehara.
1983   Local differences in plant-feeding habits of chimpanzees between the Mahale Moun-
        tains and Gombe National Park, Tanzania. Journal of Human Evolution 12:467–80.

Noble, W., and I. Davidson
1991   The evolutionary emergence of modern human behaviour: Language and its archae-
        ology. Man 26:223–53.
1993   Tracing the emergence of modern human behavior: Methodological pitfalls and a theo-
        retical path. Journal of Anthropological Archaeology 12:121–49.

Owings, D. H.
1994   How monkeys feel about the world: A review of *How Monkeys See the World*, by D. L.
        Cheney and R. M. Seyfarth. *In* Language and Communication 14(1):15–30.

Parker, S. T.
1985   A social-technological model for the evolution of language. Current Anthropology
        26(5):617–39.

Parker, S. T., and K. R. Gibson
1977   Object manipulation, tool use and sensorimotor intelligence as feeding adaptations in
        cebus monkeys and great apes. Journal of Human Evolution 6:623–41.
1979   A developmental model for the evolution of language and intelligence in early homi-
        nids. Behavioral and Brain Sciences 2:367–408.

Parker, S. T., and C. Milbrath
1993   Higher intelligence, propositional language, and culture as adaptations for planning. *In*
        Tools, Language and Cognition in Human Evolution. K. R. Gibson and T. Ingold, eds.,
        pp. 314–33. Cambridge: Cambridge University Press.

Parker, S. T., and P. Poti
1990   The role of innate motor patterns in ontogenetic and experiential development of
        intelligent use of sticks in cebus monkeys. *In* "Language" and Intelligence in Mon-
        keys and Apes. S. T. Parker and K. Gibson, eds., pp. 219–43. Cambridge: Cambridge
        University Press.

Passingham, R. E.
1982   The Human Primate. San Francisco: W. H. Freeman.
1989   The origins of human intelligence. *In* Human Origins. J. R. Durant, ed., pp. 123–36.
        Oxford: Clarendon Press.

Peoples, J., and G. Bailey
1991   Humanity: An Introduction to Cultural Anthropology. 2d ed. St. Paul: West Publishing.

Pereira, M. E.
  1988   Effects of age and sex on intra-group spacing behaviour in juvenile savannah baboons, *Papio cynocephalus cynocephalus*. Animal Behaviour 36:184–204.
Peters, A. M., and S. T. Boggs
  1986   Interactional routines as cultural influences upon language acquisition. *In* Language Socialization Across Cultures. B. B. Schieffelin and E. Ochs, eds., pp. 80–96. Cambridge: Cambridge University Press.
Peters, C. R.
  1987   Nut-like oil seeds: Food for monkeys, chimpanzees, humans, and probably ape-men. American Journal of Physical Anthropology 73:333–63.
Peters, E. H.
  n.d.   Human infancy as a vehicle for teaching anthropology. *In* Strategies for Teaching the Central Themes of Anthropology. P. Erickson, ed. New Delhi: Reliance Press. In press.
Pfeiffer, J.
  1982   The Creative Explosion. New York: Harper and Row.
Post, D.
  1978   Feeding and ranging of the yellow baboon (*Papio cynocephalus*). Ph.D. dissertation, Yale University.
  1982   Feeding behavior of yellow baboons (*Papio cynocephalus*) in the Amboseli National Park, Kenya. International Journal of Primatology 3:403–30.
Potts, R.
  1988   Early Hominid Activities at Olduvai. New York: Aldine de Gruyter.
  1991a   Untying the knot: Evolution of early human behavior. *In* Man and Beast Revisited. M. H. Robinson and L. Tiger, eds., pp. 41–59. Washington: Smithsonian Institution Press.
  1991b   Why the Oldowan? Plio-Pleistocene toolmaking and the transport of resources. Journal of Anthropological Research 47(2):153–76.
Povinelli, D. J., K. E. Nelson, and S. T. Boysen
  1990   Inferences about guessing and knowing by chimpanzees (*Pan troglodytes*). Journal of Comparative Psychology 104(3):203–10.
Povinelli, D. J., K. A. Parks, and M. A. Novak
  1991   Do rhesus monkeys (*Macaca mulatta*) attribute knowledge and ignorance to others? Journal of Comparative Psychology 105(4):318–25.
Premack, D., and G. Woodruff
  1978   Does the chimpanzee have a theory of mind? Behavioral and Brain Sciences 1:515–26.
Quiatt, D., and V. Reynolds
  1993   Primate Behaviour: Information, Social Knowledge, and the Evolution of Culture. Cambridge: Cambridge University Press.
Relethford, J.
  1990   The Human Species: An Introduction to Biological Anthropology. Mountainview, CA: Mayfield.
Rice, P. M.
  1987   Pottery Analysis: A Sourcebook. Chicago: University of Chicago Press.
Richard, A. F.
  1985   Primates in Nature. San Francisco: W. H. Freeman.
Rodseth, L., R. W. Wrangham, A. M. Harrigan, and B. B. Smuts
  1991   The human community as a primate society. Current Anthropology 32(3):221–54.
Rowell, T. E.
  1975   Growing up in a monkey group. Ethos 3:113–28.
Russon, A. E., and B. M. F. Galdikas
  1993   Imitation in free-ranging rehabilitant orangutans (*Pongo pygmaeus*). Journal of Comparative Psychology 107(2):147–61.
Sackett, J. R.
  1990   Style and ethnicity in archaeology: The case for isochrestism. *In* The Uses of Style in Archaeology. M. W. Conkey and C. A. Hastorf, eds., pp. 32–43. Cambridge: Cambridge University Press.
Savage-Rumbaugh, E. S., J. Murphy, R. A. Sevcik, K. E. Brakke, S. L. Williams, and D. M. Rumbaugh
  1993   Language comprehension in ape and child. Monographs of the Society for Research in Child Development. Serial no. 233, vol. 58:3–4.

Seyfarth, R. M.
1986   Vocal communication and its relation to language. *In* Primate Societies. B. B. Smuts, D. L. Cheney, R. M. Seyfarth, R. W. Wrangham, and T. T. Struhsaker, eds., pp. 440–51. Chicago: University of Chicago Press.
Shopland, J. M.
1987   Food quality, spatial deployment, and the intensity of feeding interference in yellow baboons (*Papio cynocephalus*). Behavioral Ecology and Sociobiology 21:149–56.
Sigg, H.
1986   Ranging patterns in hamadryas baboons: Evidence for a mental map. *In* Primate Ontogeny, Cognition, and Social Behaviour. J. Else and P. Lee, eds., pp. 87–91. Cambridge: Cambridge University Press.
Silk, J.
1978   Patterns of food sharing among mother and infant chimpanzees at Gombe National Park, Tanzania. Folia Primatologica 29:129–41.
1986   Social behavior in evolutionary perspective. *In* Primate Societies. B. B. Smuts, D. L. Cheney, R. M. Seyfarth, R. W. Wrangham, and T. T. Struhsaker, eds., pp. 318–29. Chicago: University of Chicago Press.
Simonds, P. E.
1965   The bonnet macaque in South India. *In* Primate Behavior. I. DeVore, ed., pp. 175–96. New York: Holt, Rinehart and Winston.
Slobodchikoff, C. N., J. Kiriazis, C. Fischer, and E. Creef.
1991   Semantic information distinguishing individual predators in the alarm calls of Gunnison's prairie dogs. Animal Behaviour 42:713–19.
Smith, W. J.
1977   The Behavior of Communicating: An Ethological Approach. Cambridge, MA: Harvard University Press.
Smuts, B. B.
1985   Sex and Friendship in Baboons. Hawthorne, NY: Aldine.
Smuts, B. B., D. L. Cheney, R. M. Seyfarth, R. W. Wrangham, and T. T. Struhsaker, eds.
1986   Primate Societies. Chicago: University of Chicago Press.
Snowdon, C. T.
1982   Linguistic and psycho-linguistic approaches to primate communication. *In* Primate Communication. C. T. Snowdon, C. H. Brown, and M. L. Petersen, eds., pp. 212–38. Cambridge: Cambridge University Press.
1988   Communication as social interaction: Its importance in ontogeny and adult behavior. *In* Primate Vocal Communication. D. Todt, P. Goedeking, and D. Symmes, eds., pp. 108–22. Berlin: Springer-Verlag.
1990   Language capacities of non-human animals. Yearbook of Physical Anthropology 33:215–43.
1992   The sounds of silence. Behavioral and Brain Sciences 15(1):167–68.
Snowdon, C. T., C. H. Brown, and M. L. Petersen, eds.
1982   Primate Communication. Cambridge: Cambridge University Press.
Srivastava, A.
1991   Cultural transmission of snake-mobbing in free-ranging Hanuman langurs. Folia Primatologica 56:117–20.
Stammbach, E.
1986   Desert, forest and montane baboons: Multilevel societies. *In* Primate Societies. B. B. Smuts, D. L. Cheney, R. M. Seyfarth, R. W. Wrangham, and T. T. Struhsaker, eds., pp. 112–20. Chicago: University of Chicago Press.
Stanford, C. B., J. Wallis, H. Matama, and J. Goodall
n.d.   Patterns of predation by chimpanzees on red colobus monkeys in Gombe National Park, 1982–1991. American Journal of Physical Anthropology. In press.
Stein, D. M.
1984   The Sociobiology of Infant and Adult Male Baboons. Norwood, NJ: Ablex.
Steklis, H. D.
1985   Primate communication, comparative neurology, and the origin of language reexamined. Journal of Human Evolution 14:157–73.

Strier, K. S.
1990   New World primates, new frontiers: Insights from the woolly spider monkey, or muri-qui (*Brachyteles arachnoides*). International Journal of Primatology 11:7–19.
Struhsaker, T. T.
1967   Auditory communication among vervet monkeys (*Cercopithecus aethiops*). *In* Social Communication Among Primates. S. Altmann, ed., pp. 281–324. Chicago: University of Chicago Press.
Strum, S. C.
1981   Processes and products of change: Baboon predatory behavior at Gilgil, Kenya. *In* Omnivorous Primates. R. S. O. Harding and G. Teleki, eds., pp. 255–302. New York: Columbia University Press.
1988   Social strategies and primate psychology. Behavioral and Brain Sciences 11:264–65.
Strum, S. C., and W. Mitchell
1987   Baboon models and muddles. *In* The Evolution of Human Behavior: Primate Models. W. Kinzey, ed., pp. 87–104. Albany: State University of New York Press.
Super, C. M., and S. Harkness
1986   The development of niche: A conceptualization at the interface of child and culture. International Journal of Behavioral Development 9:545–69.
Susman, R. L.
1991   Who made the Oldowan tools? Fossil evidence for tool behavior in Plio-Pleistocene hominids. Journal of Anthropological Research 47(2):129–51.
Susman, R. L., J. T. Stern, and W. L. Jungers.
1985   Locomotor adaptations in the Hadar hominids. *In* Ancestors: The Hard Evidence. E. Delson, ed., pp. 184–92. New York: Alan R. Liss.
Swartz, K. B., and L. A. Rosenblum
1981   The social context of parental behavior: A perspective on primate socialization. *In* Parental Care in Mammals. D. J. Gubernick and P. H. Klopfer, eds., pp. 417–54. New York: Plenum.
Symmes, D., and M. Biben
1988   Conversational vocal exchanges in squirrel monkeys. *In* Primate Vocal Communication. D. Todt, P. Goedeking, and D. Symmes, eds., pp. 123–32. Berlin: Springer-Verlag.
Takasaki, H.
1983   Mahale mountain chimpanzees taste mangoes: Toward acquisition of a new food item? Primates 24:273–75.
Tanner, N. M.
1981   On Becoming Human. New York: Cambridge University Press.
1987   The chimpanzee model revisited and the gathering hypothesis. *In* The Evolution of Human Behavior: Primate Models. W. Kinzey, ed., pp. 3–27. Albany: State University of New York Press.
Tappen, N. C.
1985   The dentition of the "Old Man" of La Chapelle-aux-Saints and inferences concerning Neanderthal behavior. American Journal of Physical Anthropology 67:43–50.
Teleki, G.
1973   The Predatory Behavior of Wild Chimpanzees. Lewisburg, PA: Bucknell University Press.
1974   Chimpanzee subsistence technology: Materials and skills. Journal of Human Evolution 3:575–94.
1981   The omnivorous diet and eclectic feeding habits of chimpanzees in Gombe National Park, Tanzania. *In* Omnivorous Primates. R. S. O. Harding and G. Teleki, eds., pp. 303–43. New York: Columbia University Press.
Tobias, P. V.
1987   The brain of *Homo habilis:* A new level of organization in cerebral evolution. Journal of Human Evolution 16:741–61.
Tomasello, M.
1988   The role of joint attentional processes in early language development. Language Sciences 10(1):69–88.

1990   Cultural transmission in the tool use and communicatory signaling of chimpanzees? *In* "Language" and Intelligence in Monkeys and Apes. S. T. Parker and K. R. Gibson, eds., pp. 274–311. Cambridge: Cambridge University Press.

1992   The social bases of language acquisition. Social Development 1(1):67–87.

Tomasello, M., M. Davis-Dasilva, L. Camak, and K. Bard

1987   Observational learning of tool use by young chimpanzees. Human Evolution 2:175–83.

Tomasello, M., A. C. Kruger, and H. H. Ratner.

1993   Cultural learning. Behavioral and Brain Sciences 16(3):495–552.

Tomasello, M., E. S. Savage-Rumbaugh, and A. C. Kruger

n.d.   Imitative learning of actions on objects by children, chimpanzees, and enculturated chimpanzees. Child Development. In press.

Tooby, J., and I. DeVore

1987   The reconstruction of hominid behavioral evolution through strategic modeling. *In* The Evolution of Human Behavior: Primate Models. W. Kinzey, ed., pp. 183–237. Albany: State University of New York Press.

Toth, N.

1991   Early stone technologies and linguistic/cognitive inferences. Paper given at the annual meeting of the American Association for the Advancement of Science, Washington, D.C., February.

Toth, N., K. D. Schick, E. S. Savage-Rumbaugh, R. A. Sevcik, and D. M. Rumbaugh.

1993   Pan the tool-maker: Investigations into the stone tool-making and tool-using capabilities of a bonobo (*Pan paniscus*). Journal of Archaeological Science 20:81–91.

Trinkaus, E.

1989   The Upper Paleolithic transition. *In* The Emergence of Modern Humans: Biocultural Adaptations in the Later Pleistocene. E. Trinkaus, ed., pp. 42–66. School of American Research Advanced Seminar Series. Cambridge: Cambridge University Press.

Trivers, R.

1974   Parent-offspring conflict. American Zoologist 14:249–64.

1985   Social Evolution. Menlo Park, CA: Benjamin Cummings.

Tutin, C. E. G., M. Fernandez, M. Rogers, E. A. Williamson, and W. C. McGrew

1992   Foraging profiles of sympatric lowland gorillas and chimpanzees in the Lope Reserve, Gabon. *In* Foraging Strategies and Natural Diet of Monkeys, Apes and Humans. A. Whiten and E. M. Widdowson, eds., pp. 19–26. Oxford: Oxford University Press.

Visalberghi, E.

1987   The acquisition of nut-cracking behavior by two capuchin monkeys (*Cebus apella*). Folia Primatologica 49:168–171.

1990   Tool use in cebus. Folia Primatologica 54:146–54.

Visalberghi, E., and D. M. Fragaszy

1990   Do monkeys ape? *In* "Language" and Intelligence in Monkeys and Apes. S. T. Parker and K. R. Gibson, eds., pp. 247–75. Cambridge: Cambridge University Press.

Voelker, W.

1986   The Natural History of Living Mammals. Medford, NJ: Plexus Publishing.

Walters, J.

1986   Transition to adulthood. *In* Primate Societies. B. B. Smuts, D. L. Cheney, R. M. Seyfarth, R. W. Wrangham, and T. T. Struhsaker, eds., pp. 358–69. Chicago: University of Chicago Press.

Watts, D. P.

1985   Observations on the ontogeny of feeding behavior in mountain gorillas (*Gorilla gorilla beringei*). American Journal of Primatology 8:1–10.

Westergaard, C., and D. Fragaszy

1987   The manufacture and use of tools by capuchin monkeys (*Cebus apella*). Journal of Comparative Psychology 101(2):159–68.

Whitehead, J. M.

1986   Development of feeding selectivity in mantled howling monkeys, *Alouatta palliata. In* Primate Ontogeny, Cognition, and Social Behaviour. J. Else and P. C. Lee, eds., pp. 105–17. Cambridge: Cambridge University Press.

Whiten, A., and R. W. Byrne

1988   Tactical deception in primates. Behavioral and Brain Sciences 11(2):233–74.

Whiten, A., and R. Ham
  1992   On the nature and evolution of imitation in the animal kingdom: Reappraisal of a cen-
         tury of research. *In* Advances in the Study of Behavior, vol. 21. P. J. B. Slater, J. S.
         Rosenblatt, C. Beer, and M. Milinski, eds. New York: Academic Press.
Whiting, B. B., and J. W. M. Whiting
  1975   Children of Six Cultures. Cambridge: Harvard University Press.
Wiessner, P.
  1990   Is there a unity to style? *In* The Uses of Style in Archaeology. M. W. Conkey and C. A.
         Hastorf, eds., pp. 105–12. Cambridge: Cambridge University Press.
Wobst, H. M.
  1977   Stylistic behavior and information exchange. *In* Papers for the Director: Research
         Essays in Honor of James B. Griffin. C. E. Cleland, ed. Anthropology Papers, Museum of
         Anthropology, University of Michigan 61:317–42.
Wrangham, R. W.
  1980   An ecological model of female-bonded primate groups. Behaviour 75:262–300.
Wynn, T.
  1989   The Evolution of Spatial Competence. Chicago: University of Illinois Press.
  1991   Natural history and the super organic in studies of tool behavior. *In* Interpretation
         and Explanation in the Study of Animal Behavior. M. Bekoff and D. Jamieson, eds.,
         pp. 98–117. Boulder: Westview Press.
Wynn, T., and W. C. McGrew
  1989   An ape's view of the Oldowan. Man 24:383–98.

Index

Technology, 114. *See also* Tool use
Teleki, G., 71, 72, 80
Temerin, L. A., 49
Tillier, A. M., 98
Tobias, P. V., 92, 98, 109
Tomasello, M., 80, 84, 85–86, 112, 113, 142
Tooby, J., 21, 22
Tool use, 79–80, 87; bird, 122; bonobo, 103, 121; cebus monkey, 84, 85, 87, 123–24; chimpanzee, 6, 80–84, 86, 87, 120–21, 123; early hominid, 92–93, 103–4; in extractive foraging, 119–25; gorilla, 121; *Homo erectus,* 103–4; *Homo habilis,* 103, 124; language and, 136–37; lost by apes, 121; orangutan, 86, 121; role of imitation in, 84
Toth, N., 103
Trinkaus, E., 93
Trivers, R., 29, 30–31
Tutin, C. E. G., 78

Uehara, S., 70, 80

Vandermeersch, B., 98
Vervet monkeys: alarm calls of, 44–46, 135–36; predation of, 41; referential communication by, 38–39
Visalberghi, E., 84–85, 87, 113, 123, 124
Vocal communication. *See* Communication, vocal
Voelker, W., 20

Walters, J., 33
Washburn, S. L., 21
Watts, D. P., 70, 78
Westergaard, C., 87
Whitehead, J. M., 50, 76–77
Whiten, A., 52, 53, 58, 113, 127
Whiting, B. B., 111
Whiting, J. W. M., 111
Wiessner, P., 102
Williams, S. L., 112
Williamson, E. A., 78
Wobst, H. M., 95, 102, 106
Wolkenstein, B., 43
Woodruff, G., 125–26
Wrangham, R. W., 20, 21, 23, 25, 41–42, 70, 94, 136
Wyers, E. J., 122
Wynn, T., 92, 103–4, 124

SCHOOL OF AMERICAN RESEARCH
RESIDENT SCHOLAR SERIES

Director of Publications: Joan K. O'Donnell
Editor: Jane Kepp
Designer: Deborah Flynn Post
Indexer: Andrew L. Christenson
Typographer: Tseng Information Systems, Inc.